TUNISIA

SPIRAL GUIDE

AA
Publishing

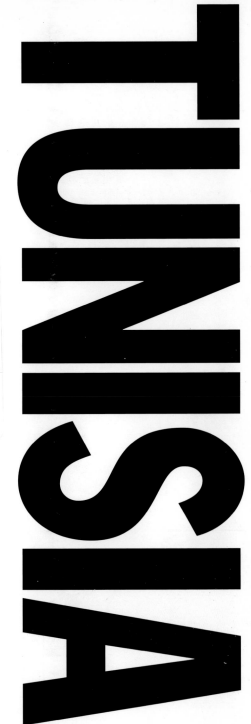

Contents

the magazine 5

Finding Your Feet 33

Around Tunis 45

The North 67

Written by Stuart Munro-Hay

Copy edited by Colin Hinshelwood
Verified by David Henley
Indexed by Andrew Forbes
Page design by Douglas E. Morton,
CPA Media, Chiang Mai, Thailand

Published by AA Publishing, a trading name of Automobile Association
Developments Limited, whose registered office is Southwood East,
Apollo Rise, Farnborough, Hampshire, GU14 0JW. Registered number
1878835.

ISBN-10: 0-7495-4364-7
ISBN-13: 978-0-7495-4364-8

The contents of this publication are believed correct at the time of
printing. Nevertheless, AA Publishing accept no responsibility for any
errors or omissions or for changes in the details given in this guide or for
the consequences of readers' reliance on this information. This does not
affect your statutory rights. Assessments of attractions, hotels, restaurants and so forth are based on the author's own experience and contain
subjective opinions that may not reflect the publishers' opinion or a
reader's experience. We have tried to ensure accuracy, but things do
change so please let us know if you have any comments or corrections.

A CIP catalogue record for this book is available from the
British Library.

Colour separation by Leo Reprographics
Printed and bound in China by Leo Paper Products

Find out more about AA Publishing and the wide range of services the
AA provides by visiting our website at www.theAA.com

We wish to dedicate this book in memory of Steve Day;
his magnificent photos remain in our library and will be a
permanent reminder of an excellent photographer with a
great personality.

A01753

the magazine

Best of
TUNISIA

Above: Historic sites are plentiful in Tunisia and details like this deeply carved entablature can be found at most of them

Below: A Maghrebi-style minaret; Kairouan has some of the finest examples of Maghrebi Islamic architecture in the world

A welcoming people living in a richly varied geographical setting, with stunning scenery ranging from forested hills and perfect beaches to deserts and oases: that is one facet of Tunisia. Add opulent Moorish architecture, the mystery and cruelty of Phoenician Carthage, and romantic Roman ruins, and you have quite enough to turn Tunisia into a delightful place to visit.

Best historic site

• If you only visit one historic site, the massive amphitheatre at **El Jem** (➤ 96) is hard to beat. It evokes the wealth of Roman Africa, the skill of its architects, and the blood and gore of the gladiatorial games and wild beast shows.

Best mosque

• If you only see one mosque, Islam's fourth holiest spot, the **Kairouan Great Mosque** (➤ 121) is the one to visit. It's vast yet elegant.

Best dish

• Tunisia's national dish, *couscous*, comes in a variety of guises and in its most refined and lavish variation merits the term *couscous royale*. Many good restaurants around the country regularly prepare this dish, but remember it can be quite spicy.

Best souq

• If you only visit one *souq* or local market, concentrate on the **Tunis Souq** (➤ 65) around the Jemma Ez Zitouna (Great Mosque). It's a fascinating hodge-podge of streets and winding alleys, with wonderfully decorated shops, people, colour and an enormous range of goods.

Best restaurant

• If you only go to one expensive restaurant, the **Dar el-Jeld** (➤ 65) in Tunis is your best choice. Not only is it in the Médina setting of an old town house, but you can dine superbly to the sound of the lute.

Best natural sights

• The breathtaking gorge at **Midès** (➤ 146) with its swirling, multi-coloured rock strata and beautiful green palm trees deep in the valley below; the constantly changing colours and shimmering mirages of the **Chott el Jerid** (➤ 136).

Best museum

• Undoubtedly the **Musée du Bardo** (➤ 60) in Tunis, one of the world's finest museums with its wonderful collection of Roman mosaics. The Carthaginian collection is also superb.

Best beach

• If you only visit one beach, and prefer the less-crowded variety, head for **Rass Sidi Ali el-Mekki** (➤ 79) near Ghar el-Melh. Soft sand, good swimming, quaint restaurants and superb views make it worth the extra effort to get there.

Top: The delightful spa town of Korbous, a small whitewashed settlement on the Cap Bon Peninsula

Above: Early morning markets are a good place to meet and mingle with Tunisians

Below: Some of the best beaches in the Mediterranean dot the Tunisian coast

The usual description for the people of Tunisia is "Arab Berber". However, over the centuries Tunisia has absorbed various waves of settlers. In 1100 BC the Phoenicians came and stayed, and their "Punic" language was still heard around Tunisia as late as AD 400. They seem to have enslaved, taxed and to some extent absorbed the native inhabitants – part Libyan, part Berber – and pointed them towards agriculture and urban settlement.

Who are the Tunisians?

Two Tribes

Once upon a time, there were two main tribes, an eastern one and a western one. They were later united under King Massinissa of Numidia (202–148 BC), who ruled from **Dougga** (➤ 116). The kingdom of Numidia, at that time, included part of Tunisia but was largely centred in Algeria. After Massinissa's death, Numidia was divided into three separate kingdoms, one of which was ruled from **Bulla Regia** (➤ 76).

The Romans

In the second century BC the Roman legions landed and began colonising the country over the next few centuries. They, in turn, were followed by the marauding Vandals in the 5th century AD, before the Romans returned to stake their claim. Meanwhile, the indigenous peoples, such as the Berbers and the Numidians, endured a nomadic life in the unforgiving desert or settled quietly along the coast.

The Arabs

Then came the Arabs, firstly in waves of conquest, but soon afterwards in the form of major tribal migrations, such as the Banu Salim and Banu Hilal (commemorated in the epic Arabic poem *Hilalia*, which is said to comprise 1 million lines). Over a prolonged period black Africans from southern regions were imported and sold at slave markets, and a Jewish community emerged. Further immigrations of other Arab or "Arabised" peoples included Muslim refugees from Sicily, who settled in the Sahel coastal region after Sicily fell to the Norman kings in 1091. More significantly, the Spanish Moors began to arrive in droves after the fall of Muslim Seville in 1248. By the early 17th century it is estimated that 200,000 Spanish Muslims had settled in the Mejerda Valley near Tunis, and on the Cap Bon peninsula in the north. Like the Phoenicians, they brought with them, as well as their blood and ancestry, new traditions, literature and superior agricultural and irrigation techniques.

The Turks

The last ethnic influence – from the 16th to the 19th century – came from the Turks, a term applying to a broad spectrum of peoples under Ottoman rule, whether European (Balkan, Greek) or Asiatic. If you add a final sprinkling of French culture to the pot, the term "Arab-Berber" seems a little simplistic. This historical crossfire of races and cultures does raise some controversial questions. For example, was Septimius Severus, the Roman emperor who came from Africa, a man of Italian colonial origin, or a black African? Whatever the case, he died in AD 211 far from the Mediterranean sunshine on the most remote Roman frontier – York in England.

Top left: A Bedouin musician at the Festival of the Sahara in Douz

Above: Relaxing with a *chicha* or water-pipe in a Tunis café

Far left: Berber women harvesting wheat near Zaghouan

Left: An Arab acrobat at the Douz Festival of the Sahara

Below: A cameleer brews tea in the desert

LAND OF COUSCOUS

Where the Maghreb Begins:

One story – perhaps true, or perhaps just an invention – goes that President Habib Bourguiba, Tunisia's first president, was once asked to define what the Maghreb was. The word in broad terms means the African lands of the west, and the people from the "sunset lands", those who follow Islam and speak Arabic but who are culturally very different from the Middle Eastern Arabs. The president is supposed to have pondered the question for a moment and then replied: "Somewhere in Libya there came a point where the eastern staple food, rice, gave way to that which defined the Maghreb – couscous."

Couscous, originally a staple food of the Berbers, has now become known far and wide as North Africa's traditional dish. The word *kuskus* is Arabic, the spelling we use – couscous – comes from French, but it all originated from the Berber word, *seksu*. This tells us that couscous was almost certainly served in the Maghreb long before the Arabs themselves arrived in the 7th century.

In the North African region many varieties of couscous have developed as different influences came into play. Tunisians are particularly fond of a well-peppered version of the dish. To make a **marga** or stew, a choice of chicken, lamb, fish or vegetables – or a mixture of these – forms the main ingredient, and is accompanied by chickpeas. It is especially delicious (for those who enjoy spicy foods) pepped up with a few splashes of the local **harissa** pepper sauce. The savoury mixture is then served on a bed of couscous – semolina grains

– often buttered to add a richer flavour, as well as helping to keep the grains from becoming lumpy. Some restaurants offer camel meat couscous as a special dish. The dish you see on menus called **couscous royale** has a particularly rich content, usually a generous mixture of lamb and chicken combined with a number of vegetables.

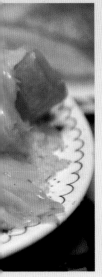

Ideally a *couscousière* is used for the preparation. This is a cleverly designed cooking vessel with two parts, the upper one pierced so that the stew in the base can provide steam for cooking the semolina above. Naturally, some of the flavour of the *marga* stew also passes into the couscous, rendering it doubly delicious. Another quite different way of serving couscous is as a sweet semolina dish enhanced with fruits, nuts and milk. This is called *mesfuf*.

Although Morocco and Algeria are equally renowned for this tasty semolina speciality, only in Tunisia are you likely to savour couscous made with seafood instead of lamb, and spiced with *harissa* before it is served. And if you ever visit the Île de Jerba, you can even try couscous with octopus.

Top: Shoppers walking between fruit and vegetable stalls in the produce market in Tunis

Above: North Africa's traditional dish comes in a choice of styles and variety of ingredients

Right: Open sacks filled with freshly ground spices and dried pulses displayed on the ground at a stall in Douz

THE PIRATES OF THE
Barbary
Coast

Piracy was once a staple form of income for the great cities of the "Barbary Coast", the shoreline of the North African Berber communities. A pirate vessel could be viewed in very different ways. Licensed British ships that preyed upon the Spanish silver fleets were heroes to the subjects of Queen Elizabeth I, but in King Philip's Spain they were simply robbers and plunderers. And vice versa, of course.

In its way, Barbary Coast "piracy" was more or less an official form of coastal policing. Enterprising ships' captains, the "Barbary corsairs" as they were infamously known, patrolled the seaways and boarded, plundered and captured any Christian vessel that passed by without the consent of the local ruler.

These pirates or corsairs operated (with their sovereigns' approval) from Tunisian ports such as Bizerte, Ghar el-Melh, La Goulette, Tunis itself, Tabarka and Île de Jerba

The Ottoman admiral, Khayr ad-Din, turned Tunis into a major centre of piracy in the 16th century

(Island of Jerba), as well as from Algiers and Tripoli. They plundered Christian shipping on the high seas, and even at times ventured to coastal raiding. Any captured sailors or passengers were either sent down to the galleys where they were whipped into shape as oarsmen, or they were taken to markets such as in Tunis and sold into slavery. The ships of the Christian nations of the time operated in exactly the same way, and on several occasions the Europeans sent fleets to confront Tunis and other coastal cities.

In 1587 – after the Ottoman sultan in Turkey had seized control over all North Africa – Tunis, Algiers and Tripoli were appointed the "Barbary regencies". They were placed under the control of local rulers entitled *dey* or *bey*, but officially they were subject to the sultan in Istanbul, to whom tribute was paid. Between 1610 and 1637 *dey* Yusuf of Tunis enthusiastically promoted piracy as a main source of income for his state. Vast numbers of Christian slaves were taken (it was estimated in 1650 that there were 35,000 of them in Algiers alone). So grievous was this situation that the Barbary pirate fleet at Porto Farina (now Ghar el-Melh) was bombarded by Oliver Cromwell's admiral, Robert Blake, in 1655.

The indignant British, French and even American governments protested constantly. Their forces tried for a long time to suppress the Barbary slavers with raids and bombardments, and in the end they succeeded. But it was not easy. In the early 1800s efforts were still continuing to suppress Tunis and

Khayr ad-Din, also known as Barbarossa, one of the most famous Barbary Coast pirates

Below: A 16th-century Genoese fort dominates the harbour of Tabarka, an ancient trading post

Red Beard!

Piracy could be good business, even the foundation of a splendid career. One Barbary corsair whose adventures led him from piracy to greatness was Khayr ad-Din, also known as **"Barbarossa"**, meaning "Red Beard". Originally a Turk, Barbarossa and his brother, Uruj opposed the Spanish and Portuguese attacks on North Africa between 1505 and 1511 and became famous for helping Muslims escape from Spain during the early years of the Spanish Inquisition.

Barbarossa took Algiers in 1529, converting the port into a stronghold of piracy in the western Mediterranean. By 1533 his achievements led to him being appointed admiral-in-chief of the Turkish navy, giving him formidable power, as well as the Ottoman Empire as support. The next year he took much of Tunisia, also turning Tunis into a major centre for piracy directed against Italy. However, this led to a retaliatory raid by the Holy Roman Emperor Charles V, resulting in the capture of Tunis and La Goulette in 1535. Nevertheless, Barbarossa assured Turkish supremacy in the eastern Mediterranean by defeating the imperial fleet at the battle of Preveza in 1538. "Redbeard" finally became a close adviser to the sultan and was buried with full honours in Istanbul after his death in 1546.

other Barbary Coast pirate states. The US navy attacked pirate bases including Tunis itself. In fact, the Americans were willing to pay for safe conduct on the Barbary Coast, regarding it as a kind of tax on the seaways, but the local *bey* made the mistake of trying to raise the prices, provoking the American navy to launch an attack on him.

By 1815–16 the *bey* of Tunis, Mohamed Bey and his fellow Barbary regents had been forced to restrict their swashbuckling ways: Tunis was bombarded in 1816 by the British, and piracy, although not completely suppressed, was certainly diminished. As a result the national income of the "pirate economies" of North Africa plummeted, and there was relatively little back-up as agriculture and trade in the region had remained modest. The supply of Christian slaves was also reduced, though African trans-Saharan slavery still flourished.

As for the fate of other Barbary corsairs, their terror of the high seas continued relentlessly, and they were even supported regularly by warring nations such as Spain, France, Britain and Holland.

The plundering, kidnapping and blackmailing declined gradually throughout the 18th century as tensions between the European Superpowers eased, and new treaties were signed to promote trade and to eradicate slavery.

Piracy along the Barbary Coast was finally extinguished by about 1830 after the French conquest of Algiers.

A battle with pirate ships off the North African coast

♦unisia's
Hall of Fame

Dido, Queen of Carthage

Along with Hannibal, Tunisia's best-known ancient character is Queen Dido, or Elissa. Legend has credited her with the illustrious role as founder of Carthage (▶ 56), perhaps as long ago as the 8th century BC. Dido was the daughter of the King of Tyre in Phoenicia (Lebanon today). When her wretched brother Pygmalion succeeded to the throne, he killed Dido's husband, Acerbas. Dido fled to North Africa with her followers. Once there, she bought land from Iarbus, the local king. As Dido's colony, Carthage, began to flourish, the jealous Iarbus threatened war unless she married him. The queen desired neither war nor Iarbus, so she prepared a funeral pyre and stabbed herself to death on it in front of her people.

That is one tale. An alternative was told by Virgil (born 70 BC) in his epic, *Aeneid*. It is the Roman poet's romantic and tragic version that has made Dido so legendary in art, music

The Death of Dido (Andrea Sacchi, 1599–1661); Queen Dido commits suicide rather than marry King Iarbus

and literature. Fleeing the destruction of Troy with his family and a few survivors, Prince Aeneas was shipwrecked near Carthage. Dido helped the distressed Trojans and soon fell in love with Aeneas. But destiny overtook them. The gods intended that Aeneas should found Rome. He was forced to depart from Carthage for Italy. Dido, despairing, killed herself. Later, in the Underworld, Aeneas glimpsed the ghostly vision of "Phoenician Dido", and tried to explain the irresistible forces that had compelled him to leave her. She would not acknowledge him: "She turned away, eyes to the ground, her face no more moved by his speech than if she stood as stubborn flint…"

Numerous works of art, music and literature exploit the theme of Dido and Aeneas, not to mention the 18th-century classical scholar, Richard Porson and his somewhat irreverent ode to Latin gerunds:

> When Dido found Aeneas would not come,
> She mourn'd in silence and was di-do-dum,

or the chilling lines of Dryden (1631–1700):

> Dido shall come, in a black Sulph'ry flame;
> When death has once dissolv'd her Mortal frame.
> Shall smile to see the Traitor vanity weep,
> Her angry Ghost arising from the Deep,
> Shall haunt thee waking, and disturb thy Sleep.

The couple are also commemorated on Dione, one of Saturn's moons, with two craters named Dido and Aeneas.

Aeneas, fleeing from Troy, dallies with the Queen of Carthage who is only too happy to dally back

Hannibal

Hannibal was the famous Carthaginian general who defied the Romans and crossed the Alps, not on skis, but on the back of an elephant.

Hannibal was born in a tent in Spain in 247 BC. He was the son of a conquering general, Hamilcar Barca, and he followed in his father's footsteps to become leader of Carthage.

Even today, Hannibal is recognised in military circles as one of the greatest strategists that ever lived. His most extraordinary exploit followed from his conviction that the best way to attack Rome was to take the war to her own doorstep.

So in the year 218 BC he set off with an army of around 40,000 men and reputedly up to 300 elephants on an epic five-month march, along the Spanish coast, the South of France, and finally through the Alps to Italy, where he would confront the shocked Roman legions.

Despite losing many men and most of his elephants in the hostile Alpine conditions, Hannibal's army ravaged the Romans, including the terrifying Battle of Cannae in 216 BC when tens of thousands of Romans died.

The Romans reacted by sending General Scipio to attack the Carthaginian mainland and Hannibal was forced to return home to defend Carthage.

Rome was spared, although history books often say that Hannibal was only a whisker away from destroying that great empire.

Hannibal was eventually defeated at Zama near Le Kef. He spent his remaining years in exile; but the Romans tracked him mercilessly for the rest of his life until he had no safe haven. He committed suicide in Turkey aged 65.

In *The Prince* (1513), the Italian statesman and writer Machiavelli notes how Hannibal kept his armies together in both good and bad times, which he suggests "…can only be accounted for by his extreme cruelty". This is not the opinion of other historians. Hannibal is said to have treated his soldiers well. An educated man who spoke four languages, even Roman records grudgingly describe him as a hero.

Habib Bourguiba

Habib ibn Ali Bourguiba (1903–2000) is one of those heroes who struggled for independence and national freedom from foreign dominance, and went from revolutionary to becoming president of his country.

Like many others in history, despite his achievements, Bourguiba's rule became autocratic, with heavy-handed "security" measures and repression of the free press and sections of society. Nevertheless, his golden statue in Tunis, and a lavish mosque and gold-domed mausoleum in his birthplace, **Monastir** (➤ 94), still stand in commemoration to him.

The corruptions of later power aside, Bourguiba really earned his reputation as a freedom fighter. After about 40 years of French control, the Destour Party attempted to implement a constitutional government in which French and Tunisians were equally represented. When France threatened to disband the movement a ground swell of public opinion rose against the colonialists.

Bourguiba was educated at an élite Tunis college and later studied law at the Sorbonne in Paris. He had already started a newspaper, *L'Action Tunisienne* in 1932, and dreamed of independence. A believer in gradual, steady change, he succeeded in mobilising support. Soon his Neo-Destour Party (NDP) counted some 80,000 members. Bourguiba organised a civil disobedience campaign in 1938 that provoked riots in Tunis, the dissolution of the NDP, and his arrest and deportation to France.

During World War II, when Germany conquered France and Tunisia, Bourguiba was handed over to Italy. Mussolini had claimed Tunisia as an Italian sphere of interest and

A detail from *Hannibal Crossing the Alps* (Jacopo Ripanda, 1490–1530)

Left: An etching of the Carthaginian general, Hannibal

Bourguiba was returned to Tunis in 1943. Meanwhile, Muhammad al-Munsif, the *bey* or monarch, had formed a nationalist government the year before, but when the Germans surrendered in Tunisia, the Free French deposed him. Bourguiba fled to Cairo, from where he observed the massive rise of protests across French North Africa.

By 1950 the French compromised, offering self-government in stages. The *bey* demanded a parliament. After an unsuccessful attempt by Tunisian ministers to state Tunisia's case for independence in the UN Security Council, disorder increased. Bourguiba, who had returned in 1949, was again arrested, along with other nationalist leaders. Unrest escalated throughout North Africa, until France finally offered full autonomy in 1954. A Tunisian government was initiated under Tahar ben Ammar; although accepted by Bourguiba, certain nationalists remained unsatisfied. A revolt flared, but was suppressed. In 1956 complete sovereignty of Tunisia was recognised, and the NDP won the first elections. Bourguiba became premier and president of the National Assembly. The following year, when the monarchy was finally abolished, he became Tunisia's first president.

Bourguiba set out to pursue a moderate political stance. Among matters he dealt with early on was the position of women. Polygamy was abolished in 1957, divorce was regulated, and women were allowed to vote. Efforts were made to improve education, health and agriculture, universities were founded, and the army was kept small. Islamic courts were abolished and schools secularised. In the 1964 elections Bourguiba's party (now called Parti Socialiste Destourien) saw its leader – the only candidate – win 96 per cent of the votes. He won again in 1969. In 1975 Bourguiba was appointed president for life. In the next years there were strikes, together with an increase in support for Islamic parties: for some, Bourguiba seemed Europeanised, not in accord with Islamic tradition. After some erratic behaviour in 1986, including the dismissal of the prime minister Muhammad Mzali, Bourguiba was removed in 1987 and declared "unfit to govern". He spent his retirement years in Monastir, and died in April 2000. His legacy as a founding father is part of the Tunisian national identity.

Independence hero and former president, Habib Bourguiba strove for the advancement of his country

Left: A bright red Tunisian flag flies proudly in the place de la Kasbah

During World War II, Tunisia was the scene of a dramatic ending to a great campaign which resulted in the German invaders being expelled from North Africa. The defeat of the German General Rommel and his Afrika Korps had long looked impossible, and the fight for Tunis proved to be a major turning point in the war.

WAR IN THE DESERT

Tunisia was witness to some of the most intense military activity in the war from November 1942 to May 1943. The Axis powers (Germany and Italy) had positioned some 20,000 troops in Tunisia by November 1942. The Allied 1st Army commanded by the British **General Kenneth Anderson** began an offensive on 25 November, but met with very strong defence. Early on 5 December the British army was halted not far from Tunis and Bizerte, and the German commander **Jürgen von Arnim** was able to secure Tunis. In hindsight, holding on to Tunis drained German resources drastically, to the detriment of the war back in Europe.

The Desert Fox

Enter one **General Erwin Rommel** – "The Desert Fox". After finally being defeated at the Battle of el-Alamein in Egypt, Rommel had retreated by January 1943 to hold on to the southern part of the eastern Tunisian coast, while his colleague von Arnim held the north. On the opposing side, General Anderson continued his attack from the west, while **Field Marshall Montgomery** pressed in with his 8th Army from the southeast. Rommel decided to attack from the west, and in mid-February the Germans ordered a major drive against the American forces between the Faid Pass in the north and Gafsa. To the west, General Heinz Ziegler's panzers destroyed 100 US tanks, prompting the Americans to retreat some 80km back.

General Erwin Rommel with some of his Afrika Corps field commanders

Rommel was ordered by Hitler to hold North Africa at all costs. He faithfully advanced not westwards to Tebessa but north from Kasserine towards Thala. But here, after pressing forward against strong American resistance in the **Kasserine Pass**, General Alexander's reserves were waiting to expel him. Rommel had lost his chance, and began to retreat. Montgomery had in the meantime been able to refortify in the west, and faced Rommel with 400 tanks and 500 anti-tank guns. His attack halted, and with the loss of 50 tanks, Rommel was recalled to Germany by Adolf Hitler in March 1943. A German national hero, feared and admired by his adversaries, Rommel was decorated and then immediately put in charge of the German defences at Normandy. He was later implicated in a conspiracy to assassinate Hitler and invited to commit suicide shortly afterwards.

Newly arrived tanks for the Afrika Korps at a North African port, 1942

Back in Tunisia, the Allies continued their offensive in mid-March, but were unable to stop the German Afrika Korps' retreating up the coast to Tunis. A British 8th Army assault on the Mareth Line near Gabès failed, but a New Zealand Corps' outflanking movement towards el-Hamma behind the German line caused the Germans to abandon the Mareth Line. In April 1943, the Afrika Korps was driven rapidly along the coastal plain north-wards toward Tunis. Instead of remov-ing the army to Sicily, the Germans, with von Arnim's army, settled on the idea of holding the area around Tunis and Bizerte.

A major offensive by Allied artillery, aircraft, infantry and tanks advanced towards Tunis on 7 May, while American and French forces similarly seized Bizerte. At Mejez el-Bab, a grain market on the site of ancient Membressa, there was a

major conflict, with many casualties. The German soldiers were cut off from retreating into the Cap Bon. Resistance collapsed, and 250,000 prisoners were taken, including General von Arnim himself.

The campaign was of considerable significance in the big picture of the war. The freeing of North Africa of all German forces not only allowed Allied shipping safe passage in the Mediterranean, but permitted the region to be used as an invasion base for Italy at a later stage. Once the Allies had secured Sicily, Mussolini's army collapsed and the Nazis were finally on the retreat.

Two members of the Afrika Korps reading letters from home

An Allied soldier stands guard over German prisoners on a North African beach

To accompany a trip to the ruins of Carthage, you might care to pack a copy of the 19th-century French writer Gustave Flaubert's extravagant historical novel *Salammbô*.

Flaubert's Salammbô

Salammbô is the name of an early settlement just south of Carthage, which according to legend, is where so many children were sacrificed and then buried in the notorious *tofet* or cemetery. Flaubert's *Salammbô* is not a place but a person: a cold, poised Phoenician beauty, sister of Hannibal, and daughter of Hamilcar Barca, the great Carthaginian generalissimo.

Flaubert pours out his dramatic and incredibly lavish descriptions of imaginary Carthaginian life during the time of the mercenaries' revolt with many memorable scenes. The characters from history are amplified with fantastically fertile imagination. Hanno, one of the ruling oligarchy in control of Carthage, is a hideous, cruel and corrupt character, who is

carried veiled in his litter into battle because he is rotting with leprosy. Narr Havas is the young king of the Numidians, a suitor of Salammbô. Salammbô herself is a devotee of the mysterious Carthaginian goddess Tanit. Matho the Libyan is her admirer and lover from afar. Finally among the chief characters comes Spendius, the cunning Greek who loathes Carthage and all it stands for, and who conspires to destroy the city.

In Flaubert's novel, drama succeeds drama. The book is filled with scenes of war, terrible cruelty and uncontrolled passion. One incident relates the theft of the sacred veil of Tanit – the soul of Carthage – from her temple. There are endless lists of treasures, perfumes and other precious things. In fact, so rich with barbaric splendour is this tale, so laden with the gleam of jewels, and the acts of the (generally rather unpleasant) leading characters, that one reviewer wrote: "the brain becomes weary of the scintillating flash of minutiae".

Don't let that discourage you. *Salammbô* may be typical of the romantic novel of the late 19th century, but Flaubert had done his research: perhaps rather too much! He knew how to tell a tale, and the book is evocative enough to be well worth reading. Even if the old Phoenician way of life is almost a caricature in the novel, and a certain license with historical fact prevails, *Salammbô* leaves a wonderful impression. Flaubert's lovely descriptions of Tunisian settings and scenery may remain with you forever after your visit here…

"Around Carthage, immobile waves glistened as the moon spread its beams on the gulf surrounded by mountains and on the lake of Tunis"

You may well wonder about the "immobile waves", but *Salammbô* is the ideal choice of book for whiling away an hour or two of leisure on some glorious Tunisian beach.

Mademoiselle Breval in the title role of the epic opera based on Flaubert's *Salammbô*

Left: Ernest Reyer, a French composer, wrote a successful opera based on Flaubert's novel

Tunisia is officially Muslim, with around 98 per cent of the population being of the Sunni persuasion. Like other religions, Islam has its bitter divisions, especially the long-standing feud between…

SUNNI

AND SHIA

IT ✦ IS ✦ SAID that in AD 632, after the death of **Muhammad**, the Prophet of Islam, Muslim leaders met at Medina in Arabia to elect a *khalifa* (successor) for the flourishing new religion. The first *khalifa* – "caliph" in English – was **Abu Bakr**, the prophet's father-in-law. **Caliph Umar** succeeded in AD 634, chosen by Abu Bakr himself and accepted by the main Muslim leaders of the time. **Uthman**, a son-in-law of Muhammad, was the third caliph, elected in AD 644 by leading Muslims. However, he was assassinated by dissidents in AD 659.

It was then that the trouble started. The fourth caliph was **Ali**, Muhammed's first cousin, who was also married to the Prophet's daughter Fatima. Their sons Hasan and Husayn carried Muhammad's own blood, and those who would later be called **Shia** – or "partisans" (of Ali) – believed that the divine right to rule was lodged in the Prophet's family. Ali's election by the people of Medina and the dissidents who had killed Uthman was opposed by a relative of Uthman, by the name of **Muawiya**. Muawiya belonged to a prominent clan called the Umayya, and he was also the governor of Syria.

The two sides came to arbitration, but some followers of Ali,

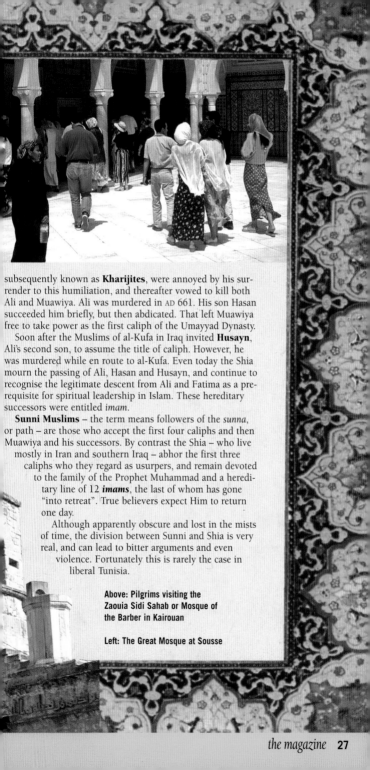

subsequently known as **Kharijites**, were annoyed by his surrender to this humiliation, and thereafter vowed to kill both Ali and Muawiya. Ali was murdered in AD 661. His son Hasan succeeded him briefly, but then abdicated. That left Muawiya free to take power as the first caliph of the Umayyad Dynasty.

Soon after the Muslims of al-Kufa in Iraq invited **Husayn**, Ali's second son, to assume the title of caliph. However, he was murdered while en route to al-Kufa. Even today the Shia mourn the passing of Ali, Hasan and Husayn, and continue to recognise the legitimate descent from Ali and Fatima as a prerequisite for spiritual leadership in Islam. These hereditary successors were entitled *imam*.

Sunni Muslims – the term means followers of the *sunna*, or path – are those who accept the first four caliphs and then Muawiya and his successors. By contrast the Shia – who live mostly in Iran and southern Iraq – abhor the first three caliphs who they regard as usurpers, and remain devoted to the family of the Prophet Muhammad and a hereditary line of 12 **imams**, the last of whom has gone "into retreat". True believers expect Him to return one day.

Although apparently obscure and lost in the mists of time, the division between Sunni and Shia is very real, and can lead to bitter arguments and even violence. Fortunately this is rarely the case in liberal Tunisia.

Above: Pilgrims visiting the
Zaouia Sidi Sahab or Mosque of
the Barber in Kairouan

Left: The Great Mosque at Sousse

The different names and words that you hear when visiting Tunisia can be confusing and often difficult to get your tongue around. Almost every foreigner agrees that Arabic is a difficult language to learn. However, that shouldn't stop you having a go: you'll have fun and you'll endear yourself to the people.

WHAT'S IN

The Arabic language of modern-day Tunisians has evolved a long way – from the sophisticated alphabet of the Phoenicians, through Latin proclamations by Julius Caesar, to the nasal pronunciation of the French Foreign Legion.

The Phoenician Alphabet

The Phoenicians first settled as traders on the Tunisian landscape about 3,000 years ago. They brought with them from what is now Lebanon an alphabet of 22 letters, which was later adopted by the Greeks, then the Romans, and could therefore be called our "Mother Alphabet".

The Phoenician city-state of **Carthage** (► 56) dominated the Tunisian coast. The name Carthage has its origins in the Phoenician term *kart hadasht* or "new city", which in Latin translated as *Carthago*.

About half of present-day Tunisia came under

A 5th-century BC Phoenician inscription on gold plate

A NAME?

Carthaginian rule, especially the fertile plains and coastal regions. At the same time, partly in Tunisia but also in Algeria, the kingdom of Numidia existed. The Numidians became known by the Arabs as *Berbers*, which, like the Roman word *Barbarian*, was directed at "uncivilised foreigners".

Later, during the height of the Roman Empire, Tunisia was simply referred to as Africa. After the conquest of Carthage, *Africa Proconsularis* comprised parts of Tunisia and the Libyan area around Tripoli. When the province was conquered by Julius Caesar in 46 BC and united with Numidia, the Romans decided to designate this new country *Africa Nova*. Stuck with Roman terminology, the Arabs referred to this colonised state as *Ifriqiya*.

A clearly lettered international road sign indicating Carthage

Arabic

The form of Arabic spoken nowadays in North Africa is known as Maghrebi Arabic, and is characterised by its lack of vowels, which can make pronunciation difficult, but certainly fun for the tourist to practise. For example, the Arabic word *médina* (city) is pronounced as *mdina*, and the name Salim comes out as *Slim*.

French

In modern times, French has left a strong influence upon the written style of the language. For instance, the Arabic term for "market", *suq*, was rendered in French as "souq", and names like this are immortalised by street signs, maps and guide books. You can quickly work out that *al-Qayrawan* is Kairouan (*al* is the Arabic for "the"). However, you might have to think for a minute before you realise that **Sfax** is derived from *al-Safaqus* – a fine example of Maghrebi vowel-suppression and French spelling in harmony. And how many visitors are likely to guess that *Bu Ruqaybah* is actually Bourguiba, the late president of Tunisia?

Mosaics are the striking legacy of Roman occupation

More than any other country within the Roman Empire, Tunisia developed to a refined art the technique of making attractive flooring out of tiny pieces of different coloured stone: a system now known as…

MOSAIC ART

Even in old Carthaginan sites like Kerkouane, long before the Romans conquered the country, local people were designing simple coloured pebble flooring in their houses. One particular floor design consisted of a reddish base flecked with white stones, and directly in front of the doorway as a protection against evil influences – the Tanith symbol, a triangle topped with a line and a circle. More complex floors of mosaic *tesserae* (small square coloured stones) with neat borders laid out in white, black and red have been found at Carthage itself, dating back to the 4th century BC.

After the Romans arrived the technique came to its greatest glory. Roman citizens in towns like *Neapolis* (Nabeul), *Hadrametum* (Sousse), *Taparura* (Sfax), *Thaenae* (Thina), *Thysdrus* (El Jem), Carthage and Bulla Regia, among many others, grew rich from trading in local products. They built beautiful villas for themselves and their families. To display their wealth and generosity, nobles would sponsor great public buildings as well: a forum, baths, a gymnasium or a theatre perhaps. These structures were built with costly marble, and floored with the best of the region's mosaics. Distinct mosaic schools developed, and some mosaics were designed in duplicate, so that citizens could go and choose their own favourite pattern at the workshop.

After the decline of the great cities, many floors remained more or less intact beneath collapsed roofs and ceilings. They were covered by sand drifts or deposits of earth, and protected for some 1,500 years.

Many of these tiled floors have been recovered and are displayed at museums such as the **Bardo** (➤ 60) in Tunis, and the museum in the *kasbah* at **Sousse** (➤ 93). If you get a chance to visit, you cannot help but be impressed by these examples of mosaic artwork from between the 2nd and the 7th centuries AD. One aspect of particular interest is the way the local life of the area is depicted. By the 3rd century mosaic scenes were becoming common in private as well as public buildings. The workshops of North Africa must have laboured overtime to fill the demands of the rich for more and more opulent compositions. They developed a pure "African" style not found elsewhere, skilled and richly varied in themes. You can see farmers and villa owners (some even have names) amid scenes from country life, hunting, war, the circus, local flora and fauna, aquatic creatures, and the exotic tales from Greek and Roman mythology.

In the later Byzantine tomb mosaics the style has changed. You might find a pictorial view of a church, or a figure of the deceased, with inscriptions giving his/her name and date of

A mosaic depicting the sea god Oceanus, dating from about the 2nd century AD

death. You can also read how the medieval Tunisians pronounced their Latin: *in bace* instead of *in pace*, meaning "in peace".

Among the most famous of all is the mosaic showing Ulysses, bound to the mast of his ship, listening to the seductive song of the Sirens; and another with a portrait of Virgil, author of the *Aeneid*, and its tragic tale of Dido, Queen of Carthage. Both are on display at the Bardo. Impressive for their size (some were required to fill the floor space of very substantial rooms), are tremendous works centred on Neptune, God of the Sea, amid a flurry of sea creatures, perfect adornments for the seaside villas of the Roman rich.

The mosaic art of Tunisia is especially valuable today since it is the only art form which shows us the way of life of the people of that glorious era.

A macabre theme: A Roman contemplates a severed head

The very best places to see mosaics

• The **Bardo Museum** in Tunis (➤ 60). Vast and splendid, the Bardo hosts the best collection of mosaic artwork in the world.
• Most elegantly presented are those in the **Musée de Sousse** in Sousse *kasbah* (➤ 93).
• Another very good collection with a lot of local material is in the **Sfax Musée Archéologique** (➤ 99).
• Mosaics still in their original setting can be seen at most of the Roman sites.

Finding Your Feet

First Two Hours

On arriving at Tunis-Carthage Airport or any other international airport in Tunisia, you will need to go through Customs and the usual passport control.

Arriving by Air

- On arrival all foreign visitors to Tunisia are issued with **landing cards** in which your passport details, etc should be filled in. This card remains with you until your departure, when it is collected at the exit point.
- If you come from the **EU**, the **United States**, **Canada** or **Japan**, you **do not require a visa**. In case these laws change, it might be a good idea to check with a Tunisian Embassy or reliable travel agent before departure.
- You can enter Tunisia with **a maximum of**: 1 litre of spirits or 2 litres of wine; 400 cigarettes; two cameras and one video camera.

Tunis-Carthage Airport

The airport is a spacious modern building decorated with a lot of granite and marble designed in a neo-Moorish style.

- **Cash point machines** for the main credit cards like **Visa** and **MasterCard** are conveniently located.
- **Currency exchange** booths, or *bureaux de change* are available in the Arrivals Lounge. You'll need to change at least some money into **Tunisian dinars (TD)** immediately unless you are being escorted directly to your hotel by a tour company.
- **Car rental** offices such as Avis, Hertz and many others are situated within the terminal building.

From the Airport to Tunis

- The airport is only **7km** from the Tunis city centre. There are also routes going directly from the airport to the **Carthage/La Marsa** area, to **Bizerte**, or to the **south**, without having to enter Tunis.
- **Yellow taxis** (make sure the meter is on or that a price has been agreed in advance) are the simplest method of getting to the city and elsewhere.
- It costs around **3 dinars** to get to Tunis. Add a small supplement if you have a lot of luggage, and remember that a 50 per cent standard extra charge is added in the evening and at night.
- **Private taxis** without meters should either be avoided, or the price agreed firmly before getting in.
- If you speak French (or Arabic) the taxi drivers can be a **mine of information** about places you might later want to visit.
- **Bus No. 35** can take you to avenue Habib Bourguiba, the main artery of the new town of Tunis. A more expensive option is the **Transtours** service that runs from the airport to the main railway station on the place de Barcelone (situated not far from avenue Habib Bourguiba). The bus runs every half hour, 6 am–midnight, and once every hour the rest of the night.

Monastir-Skanès Airport

The Monastir-Skanès Airport is 10km west of Monastir. Most visitors are generally part of a **package tour** where the formalities of arrival and onward transport are looked after by the company couriers. However, if you are travelling independently:

- There is a Sahel **metro station** just outside the airport, which offers a service between **Sousse** and **Mahdia** via Monastir and Skanès Airport.
- **Yellow taxis** cost about 6 dinars to Monastir.

Arriving by Boat

In the case of arrivals at the ferry port of **La Goulette**, the Customs formalities and use of taxis do not differ much from those described above.

Information about Tunisia

On arrival at the airport you may want to make reservations or check facts and figures. There is usually an internet café open at Tunis-Carthage Airport. These are some recommended websites for visitors:

www.tourismtunisia.com
www.focusmm.com/tunisia/tn_toumn
http://en.marweb.com/tunisia
www.lonelyplanet.com/destinations/africa/tunisia
www.planetware.com/free/cltun.htm

Tourist Information Offices

Tunisian National Tourism Office (ONTT)
Tunis Headquarters
⊞ 179 F3
✉ 1 avenue Mohammed V
☎ (71) 341077; fax: (71) 350997;
ontt@Email.ati.tn,
info@tourismtunisia.com

Bizerte
⊞ 181 D4
✉ 1 rue de Constantinople
☎ (72) 432897

Gabès
⊞ 183 D3
✉ avenue Hedi Chaker
☎ (75) 270254

Hammamet
⊞ 181 E3
✉ avenue Habib Bourguiba
☎ (72) 280423

Kairouan
⊞ 181 D2
✉ avenue de la République
☎ (77) 231897

Monastir
⊞ 181 E2
✉ rue de L'Indépendence
☎ (73) 461960

Sousse
⊞ 181 E2
✉ avenue Habib Bourguiba
☎ (73) 225157

Tabarka
⊞ 180 B4
✉ boulevard 7 Novembre
☎ (78) 671491

Tozeur
⊞ 182 A3
✉ Abou el-Kacem el-Chabbi
☎ (76) 454088

Dangers and Annoyances

On the whole Tunisia is a very safe place to visit, and you are unlikely to encounter any dangers on your arrival or indeed throughout your stay. Annoyances are another matter, however. Be on the look out for **hustlers** and **false guides**, both at the airports and at La Goulette port. These dubious entrepreneurs may tell you there is no public transport into town in the hope that you will take their car, or that your hotel has recently closed – however, surprise – they know another place which is even better, cheaper and more conveniently located. Be **polite but firm** in declining such services and head straight for the **airport information office** instead. Fortunately there are relatively few of these nuisances at Tunisia's international airport and ferry port.

Getting Around

Tunisia, especially Tunis and its region, is quite well served with public transport of all sorts.

Tunis Area

- The main **bus station** is on place de Barcelone. The public buses and the private green and white city buses (more expensive but seated passengers only, so less crowded) serve a large area of the capital. They can be difficult for tourists to use as there is no bus map, and the numbers are normally written in Arabic. You buy your ticket on board.
- The **metro** is a good modern tram system now running on five lines. The end destination is usually written at the front in both Arabic and English. The main station is at place de Barcelone.
- The **TGM** (Tunis-Goulette-Marsa) train is wonderfully convenient for touring around Tunis, serving the northern suburbs, and passing through Carthage (several stations) and Sidi Bou Saïd. Trains depart from the Tunis Marine Station at the end of avenue Habib Bourguiba, which also serves Metro Line 1. There are two classes, 1st and 2nd. Tickets should be bought before boarding. The trains continue until 3am, and run about every 15 minutes.
- **Taxis** are not too expensive in Tunis. The yellow ones with a blue disc on the door are the official ones with a meter. The driver should either use this meter, or arrange a price in advance, otherwise you risk problems at your destination. As in any large city, there can be difficulties finding a free taxi during rush hour. Evening travel is 50 per cent more expensive.

Transport in Tunisia
Internal Flights

- From Tunis, internal **Tunisair** (boulevard du 7 Novembre, 2035 Tunis-Carthage, tel: 71 700100) flights serve a selection of airports around the country: Jerba, Monastir, Sfax, Gabès, Tozeur and Tabarka.
- The airports are also served by two smaller airlines, **Tuninter** (6 rue de l'Artisanat, 2035 Tunis-Carthage, tel: 71 701717) and **Tunisavia** (route de l'Ariana, 2035 Tunis-Carthage, tel: 71 717600). During the high season it is better to book in advance, as the demand is high and the planes rather small.

Trains

- Relatively cheap **trains** of the national SNCFT (Societé Nationale des Chemins de Fer Tunisiens) system serve a network of lines throughout Tunisia from the main station at place de Barcelone.
- Second class is **generally crowded**, first class less so, and there is a more comfortable *confortable* class.
- Trains are not particularly fast, but are **reasonably efficient**.
- There is sometimes an **extra supplement** for fast trains.

Intercity Buses

- **Buses are less expensive** than the trains, and there is a good system, but early booking is best as they tend to fill up quickly. Some intercity buses are now quite comfortable, with air-conditioning.
- The National Intercity Bus Company, **SNTRI**, timetables are printed in the French-language newspapers *Le Temps* and *La Presse*.

- Tunis has different bus terminals for different regions. **Bab Saadoum** for the north, and **Bab el-Fellah** for the south and west (and Libya).

Shared Taxis (*Louages*)

- This **excellent system** is popular throughout Arab countries. The cars are **large saloons** that take five passengers, the cost shared by all.
- These *louage* (rent) taxis can be found beside the main bus stations at Bab Saadoum and Bab el-Fellah, and when there are enough people to go to a particular city, the car leaves.
- If you are scared by drivers with a certain **taste for speed**, stay with the bus or train.

Car Rental

- This is perhaps **the best way** to see the country in a relatively short time. The main sites can be seen in a week or ten days of relatively easy driving.
- The **minimum age** for renting a car is **21**. You will need to produce your **passport** and **driving licence**, and **credit cards** are accepted.
- You'll pay around 575 dinars to rent **a modest car for ten days** and will have to leave a refundable deposit.
- Ensure the **condition** of the car and the **petrol level** are noted beforehand, otherwise you might be asked to pay for extras when you return it.
- Booking can be done by **Internet** in advance for the main companies. Try: www.cheap-car-rentals-in.com/tunisia.htm
- Reliable cars are available from **Avis** (tel: 71 782077), **Europcar** (tel: 71 340303), **Hertz** (tel: 71 248559) and **Topcar** (tel: 71 285003).

Driving in Tunisia

- There are not that many cars on the roads in Tunisia, although traffic in the main cities is always increasing. British drivers in particular should remember that **driving on the right** can be confusing if you are not used to it.
- Speed limit on motorways: **110kph**
- Speed limit on main roads: **90kph**
- Speed limit on urban roads: **50kph**
- *Seat belts* are not compulsory and only modern vehicles appear to have them fitted.
- **Petrol** is cheap by European standards and costs the same everywhere. It is sold as super, regular and *sans plomb* (lead-free).
- One local road rule which can cause the uninitiated a lot of problems is the French practice of **giving way to traffic coming from the right** in built-up areas. This applies, confusingly, to smaller roads and even on round-abouts (traffic circles), where you must give way to traffic coming from the right **even if you are already on the roundabout**.
- Tunisia has plenty of **traffic police** who enforce road rules strictly, though they are certainly more lenient to foreign visitors than to locals. Treat them with respect and **act politely** if you are pulled over and you will almost certainly get away with a friendly warning.

Admission Charges
The cost of admission for museums, sites and places of interest mentioned in the text is indicated by the following price categories:

Inexpensive under TD3   **Moderate** TD3–TD5   **Expensive** over TD5

Accommodation

In a country that has for more than 40 years promoted tourism as a significant part of the national budget, accommodation for visitors is naturally quite well-developed.

There is a theoretical star rating for accommodation, laid down by the National Office for Tourism, which rates standards for hygiene, safety and service. However, general opinion suggests that this rating system has become unreliable and obsolete.

Three seasons are recognised: High (July to mid-Sep); Middle (Apr–Jun); and Low (Nov–Mar).

Zone Touristique

- This system, literally **tourist zone**, has grown over recent years in specified areas usually a few kilometres from an old city, taking advantage of some favourable spots endowed with superb beaches. You will see this in many places around the country.
- In its way, the *zone touristique* system has been a **practical solution** to indiscriminate building, as the infrastructure of airports, roads, transport, electricity, water, food supplies, beach facilities and so on, could be developed to serve mass needs. The **hotels** themselves offer almost everything you might need: room and board, restaurants and bars, facilities for watersports, tennis, tourist shops.
- If you want something from "outside" – **golf, car rental** or **excursions**, for example – the hotel can arrange these too. The older cities are therefore left practically undisturbed.
- Several older cities have **nests of modern hotels**, often near their *médinas*, built in the early days of tourism before the zone idea.

Luxury Hotels

- In Tunis, Hammamat, Sfax, Sousse and Port El Kantaoui, for example, you will find **luxury hotels** of international standard, as well as some surprising discoveries inland like The Kasbah at Kairouan, actually built to fill the town's old *kasbah*.

All-inclusives

- On the coast the usual form is the **package tour hotel**, many of which have sprouted up at each resort in the *zones touristique*.
- These areas are usually quite **well signposted** from the approaches to the towns and hotels seem, in general, to be in the 3-star category.
- **Individual travellers** who arrive without making reservations will usually find that they are charged a higher price than package holidaymakers.

Mid-range Hotels

- Independent visitors who want something in the way of a **comfortable mid-range hotel** can find such accommodation in Tunis and all the coastal resorts, with new hotels also being developed at Gammarth, Bizerte and Tabarka.
- There are a few good mid-range hotels in some inland spots too, such as Tozeur, Nefta and Douz, where they cater for **visitors to the desert** regions.
- There are a number of good mid-range hotels on the **island of Jerba** in the far south.

Budget Accommodation

- **Budget hotels** and **guest houses** are often found in the *médinas* of the older cities, or in the new towns built round them.
- They vary in quality, but whichever you choose you will find them much more **in touch with the country and people**, and within a stone's throw of the markets, shops and cafés.
- **Beware** though, many of these places are somewhat scruffy, security of valuables is less certain, hygiene and comfort might be minimal, and the possibility of noise and creepy-crawlies may be too much for some visitors.

Touring Club *Marhalas* and *Caravanserais*

- The **Touring Club de Tunisie** runs a chain of *marhalas* (cheap, traditional hotels). These exploit traditional buildings such as the **troglodyte dwellings** in Matmata, a **ksar** (originally fortified granary) at Metameur, or one of the splendid *caravanserais* converted to hotels at Houmt Souk in Jerba.
- *Caravanserais* are the legacy of lodgings where **caravans of camels** used to stop overnight on their journeys between the major trading towns of North Africa.

Camping

- Campsites are few and facilities are poor in Tunisia. There are **no official campsites** and very few places to buy equipment.

Hostels

- There are several **youth hostels** in Tunisia, known as *auberges de jeunesse*, normally located in the *médinas* of the main cities or near coastal towns where all-inclusive hotels do not prevail.
- Hostels are invariably **inexpensive** and there is no age limit. Accommodation is often in dormitories and there may be a restaurant and other facilities.
- Most youth hostels operate a strict "curfew", locking up **before midnight** (check at the reception desk). Segregation of the sexes is also carefully, if politely, insisted on.

Booking Accommodation

- If you do not have a hotel arranged before you arrive or you are planning to view other areas, you should **check these websites** for information and online bookings:
  www.expedia.co.uk/daily/hotels/Tunisia.asp
  www.southtravels.com/africa/tunisia
- Sometimes this system is **not 100 per cent reliable**. For instance, the Grand Hotel du Lac in Tunis is now closed but still appears on reservations lists. So, if you don't get a prompt acknowledgement, try elsewhere.
- Finding adequate and even good accommodation without booking presents **little problem** in the low season between December and March, but at other times it makes good sense to book ahead.

Accommodation Prices
The prices below are for a standard double room per night.

£ under TD50   ££ TD50–TD100   £££ over TD100

Food and Drink

Food in Tunisia is plentiful and delicious, but not very varied. Exotic restaurants are rare, with Italian perhaps the most adventurous, except for the odd Chinese or Thai restaurant in an up-market resort. There is usually only a choice between Tunisian and "international cuisine". The former you will find in the *souqs* (markets) and smaller towns, the latter in the hotels catering more or less exclusively for tourists.

Restaurants and *Rotisseries*

- You will find a selection of restaurants in most small towns. Those that use the French word *restaurant* may not be too surprised to see a foreigner enter. However, you might inspire looks of astonishment if you walk into a small local *rotisserie* (aimed at working men, usually with a rotating spit of roasting chickens outside) or a *gargotte* (where a wider choice is served). The welcome is all the more warm for that.
- **Bread** is traditionally eaten with every meal (the local type is called *hubz*), using the right hand only.

Tunisian Cuisine

- A legacy of French colonialism means that you can always find European-style food, however, the delicious **local dishes** are well worth trying.
- Some of the French imports have been "Tunisified", and you will find **baguettes** richly spread with *harissa* (a hot chilli paste) and containing egg, tuna, olives, tomato, lettuce and boiled potato, or the *fricassé*, which is basically the same but in a smaller *beignet* (doughnut) form.
- Fish, especially tuna, and eggs are basics, as are olives and fresh bread as **hors d'oeuvres**, usually served with *harissa* to liven them up a bit.
- The **olives** are excellent, whether the younger green or the mature black. After harvesting around November, they are soaked in brine and then transferred into a marinade of olive oil, herbs, garlic, lemon and the spicy *harissa*.
- **Brik** is an excellent egg dish that makes a good starter. It consists of a thin, crisp, pastry case or folded pancake rather like an enlarged *samosa*, but with a lightly cooked egg inside. Herbs, prawns, tuna and other seafood can provide extra flavour in the filling. *Brik* is not necessarily the easiest thing to eat: it requires either speed or patience. There is a tendency for the egg to pop out vigorously when you attack the case unless you choose the correct angle.
- Another egg dish is **chakchouka** or **ojja**, rather like a stuffed omelette but made with poached or scrambled eggs accompanied by capsicum, peppers, garlic and tomatoes. Brains, **merguez** sausage or prawns can accompany the *ojja*.
- Hard-boiled eggs and tuna accompany **mechouia**, which is a grilled mixture of chopped onions, capsicums and tomatoes, then laced with olive oil.
- Typical Arab dishes include a spicy aubergine dip, **hummus bi tahinah**, a paste of ground chick peas and sesame eaten with bread; **tabbulah**, the popular mixed salad of onions, tomatoes, radishes, parsley and mint; and **kofta**, fried meatballs served with chopped liver, peppers and onions.
- **Lablabi** is a good thick chick pea soup; and another, called **chorba** (from the Arabic word *sharaba* – to drink – from which we get our "sherbet"),

is made with pasta granules, tomatoes and onions enhanced with spicy *harissa*.

■ *Harissa* is used in the delicious national dish of the North African Arab Berber lands, ***couscous*** (➤ 10).

■ A dish that has also become popular in France is the ***mechoui***, a grillade of lamb or other meat with liver, and the spicy sausage called ***merguez***, all laced with chopped chillies.

Sweets and Desserts

■ Apart from the French-style *pâtisseries* found here and there, you will see piles of small sweet, sticky pastry cases with a variety of fillings in the local markets. These include ***makroud***, stuffed with dates, and ***kab al-ghazal*** (gazelle horn) filled with almond paste and honey.

■ There are also the various types of equally sweet and sticky ***baklava***, filo-pastry with honey and lemon juice, walnuts or pistachios, and sometimes spices such as cardamom, cloves or cinnamon.

■ **Dates**, on their own or stuffed with marzipan, are another delicacy, from the oases of the desert south.

Wine, Beer and Liqueurs

■ **Local wines** are popular and easily obtainable. *Vieux Magon* is a fruity red, as is *Sidi Saad* in its green glass jug. There are also plenty of others varying in price. A fresh dry *Blanc de Blanc* is also available, with a range of other white wines, along with rosés, like *Gris de Tunisie*.

■ There are also light **lager beers**, the German *Berbere*, made in Hammamet, and the Tunisian, *Celtia*.

■ Among stronger drinks are ***Thibarine***, a very sweet liqueur made from dates in the village of Thibar situated in the Teboursouk Mountains near Dougga, and a local "brandy" made from figs called ***boukha***.

■ Most Tunisians practice a **moderate and tolerant** form of Islam, but alcoholic beverages remain officially *haram* (forbidden) under Islamic Shari'a law, so it's both **polite and sensible** to restrict consumption of alcohol to licensed premises. Public drinking – and certainly public intoxication – are socially unacceptable.

Juices, Coffee and Tea

■ Fruit juices are readily available, as well as a local **lemon** drink called *boga*, and some sticky and sweet *sirops* (some rather exotic, like **pomegranate**, **almond milk** or **mint**). If you don't have a "sweet tooth", you might want to dilute these drinks with bottled mineral water.

■ Coffee is the standard hot drink in cafés, including delicious **Turkish-style coffee** with cardamom (very sugary), and *chai bi'nana*, refreshing **mint tea**, often drunk as an accompaniment to a water-pipe or *chicha* filled with the tobacco-like leaf of the *tombac*, and mixed with honey and lemon.

Restaurant Prices
Prices in this book are based on the amount you should expect to pay per person for a standard three-course meal, excluding drinks and service charges.

£ under TD15   ££ TD15–TD30   £££ over TD30

Shopping

What should you buy in Tunisia? And where? Some of the best places to shop are the *souqs* (local markets), the heart of the old *médinas* of Tunisian medieval cities. Passing under the vaulted arches of the *souq*, you will find yourself strolling into a maze of ancient alleyways and browsing a colourful variety of market stalls.

Where to Go

- The *souqs* are intriguing areas where there are fascinating things to see, smell and hear. They still mainly keep to the old arrangement of one street for one trade. Most open early but some may close for a two-hour lunch, then reopen.
- If you don't have time or the inclination, or simply want to learn approximate prices, the **Offices Nationales de l'Artisanat Tunisien** (ONAT: a national handicraft administration which has offices in most large towns) have fixed and marked prices, at the higher end of the scale, but with a possible edge on quality.

What to Buy

- Tunisia is rich in handicrafts. **Carpets** and **textiles** are a popular buy; they form the centre point of the traditional room, where people sit on cushions arranged around carpets. If you are buying something large and valuable, like a quality carpet, be sure that you get a proper receipt to facilitate matters at Customs should any questions be asked.
- Tunisian-style **costumes** make excellent souvenirs. For men there are light cotton *jellabas* (long robes), heavier woollen *burnus*, and *chechias* or red woollen fez-style hats decorated with little gilded ornamental designs. For women there are traditional designs altered with some concessions to modern fashions. **Silk scarves** are popular too, as are the exotic **perfumes**.
- **Ceramics** are another of Tunisia's specialities. You can buy vessels of all shapes and sizes, decorated with a wide range of traditional designs, or specially painted to order, as well as tile work – perhaps an exotic "Moorish" panel of several tiles.
- **Jewellery** and **metalwork** are essential Tunisian accessories. In Tunisia, the gold is not of very high quality, perhaps 12- to 14-carat, and the "silver" is usually plated metal, but the designs are very attractive; a **Hand of Fatima**, perhaps, or a silver fish. Some of the Berber jewellery consists of heavy silver ornaments, usually decorated with semi-precious stones.
- **Copper** workers throng the *souqs* of several old *médinas*. The craftsmen can personalise items for you. Plates, trays, lamps, coffee pots and smaller items are available. A **water-pipe** (*chicha*) makes an attractive souvenir.
- Items carved from **olive wood** can be found in Sfax, the land of the olive groves.
- **Leatherwork** is another good deal in Tunisia – **pouffes** (easily folded small for transport), *babouche* slippers, wallets, bags and even stuffed leather camels. Check the quality of workmanship before buying.
- And finally…always remember that this is Tunisia and that **haggling** is expected in marketplace situations. It's not considered rude or mean, and is all part of the fun. Try to enjoy the sport – and a cup or two of mint tea along the way.

Entertainment

Clubs and Discos

- The larger hotels, and a few of the more up-market restaurants in the capital, are the main sources of nightlife, with their **discos** and **cabaret shows** (➤ 66). There are also a few large **modern nightclubs** in Tunis, Hammamet, Sousse and some of the other main tourist destinations.
- **Discothèques** and **piano-bars** are quite popular in Tunis and the prosperous suburban seaside resorts of La Marsa and Gammarth, almost all of them in hotels.

Casinos

- A number of **casinos** can be found in Tunis and the resorts popular with tourists; the **Casino Emeraude** (tel: 72 278655), Hammamet; **Grand Casino** (tel: 75 757537), Jerba; **Casino Club Caraibe** (tel: 73 211777), Sousse.
- To gain entry you will need to be **over 21** and non-Muslim, so take your passport.

Cabaret

- Some restaurants offer **local music** and **dance shows**. These include such feats as balancing large jugs or several different breakable items on the head. This forms a staple of hotel cabaret entertainment. There is usually a small local orchestra playing traditional Tunisian music, and a girl or two dancing, dressed in traditional costume.
- Occasionally cabarets will include **snake charmers** and **belly dancers**, although it is rare these days to see a genuine belly dancer.

Cafés and Eating Out

- Tunisians themselves seem to prefer sitting and chatting in the **pavement cafés** over coffee and a water-pipe, watching the world pass by.
- An alternative is to **dine out** at one of the lovely towns along the coast, like La Marsa, Goulette or Gammarth (➤ 61).

Cultural Shows and Festivals

Traditional culture shows usually take place at the numerous festivals throughout the country. Information and dates about the many local festivals that are now staged annually in Tunisia can be obtained from the local tourism offices or via the Internet; one particularly good site is www.g-koba.com/mapas_tun.htm.

- Festivals vary enormously in style, with each region in the country offering something different: from the northern Tabarka Coral Festival in **July** to the Tozeur Folklore Festival and the Douz National Sahara Festival in **December** in the desert south.
- Regional **wine** and **falconry festivals** are held in the Cap Bon region.
- Midoun on the island of Jerba features imitation **Berber wedding processions**, and in the desert area you can witness huge gatherings of Bedouin and nomads with **camel** and **horse-riding shows**.

Theatre and Cinema

- There are standard **music concerts** and **theatrical performances** in some of the larger cities such as Tunis and Hammamet. Emperor Hadrian's restored theatre at Carthage features some mega-spectaculars, including cinema, theatre, dance and music.

- Tunis has several theatres, the most prominent being the **Théâtre Municipal** with its elegant façade on avenue Habib Bourguiba (➤ 66). Concerts of Arabic and European classical music are staged here.
- Details of the **programmes** here and at the three or four other smaller theatres in town can be obtained at the tourism office.
- There are many **cinemas** on or just off Tunis' avenue Habib Bourguiba, in the Nouvelle Ville, with the emphasis being on modern American movies (➤ 66).

Golf
- Golf is very popular, and has been quite heavily invested in by the Tunisians. This has resulted in some **excellent facilities** at several of the coastal resorts, such as Hammamet, El Kantaoui, Skanès and Tunis (Carthage).

Watersports
- Given Tunisia's splendid coasts and plentiful beaches and islands, there are dozens of watersports centres at the resorts, including **diving** sites (especially at Tabarka), and marinas for **sailing** (El Kantaoui, Bizerte, Monastir, Sidi Bou Saïd, Tabarka and La Goulette).
- **Swimming** and **sea fishing** are catered for in many places, the former either at the beaches or in hotel pools, the latter at many ports where you can rent a boat.
- **Tennis** and **riding**, like swimming, are possible for a small fee at hotels with these facilities.

Football and Other Sports
- Football is the **most popular spectator sport** in the country. Tunisia became the first African team to win a World Cup Finals match when they beat Mexico 3–1 in 1978. Tunisia also qualified for the World Cup in 1998 and 2002. More recently, the country not only hosted but won the African Cup of Nations in 2004, so the topic of football can open doors to endless conversations with locals.
- If you would like **to see a match**, simply ask the staff at your hotel. The Tunisian season runs from October to the end of March and games are usually played on Saturday and Sunday afternoons.
- Like it's Maghrebi neighbours, Morocco and Algeria, Tunisia is hooked on **middle- and long-distance running.** You will see plenty of aspiring young athletes out running in the streets. Don't be afraid to join them.
- **Volleyball** is also very popular, both on hard courts and at the beach. All-in resorts may put on volleyball competitions.

Other Entertainment
- At Sousse, the Hergla Park provides a **Go-Kart circuit**, where you can both rent or watch demonstrations.
- For those who like **bowling**, there are facilities at Les Berges du Lac, Tunis, and at the Centre Commerciale at La Marsa.
- There are several **tennis clubs** in the Tunis area, such as the Tennis Clubs of Carthage, Salammbô and Tunis.
- **Horse riding** is possible at Club Hippique at La Soukra, near La Marsa.
- **Hunting** and **shooting** are mainly mountain sports which take place in the wooded hills of the north around Ain Draham and Tabarka, in the Khroumir Mountains. Wild boar are especially prized. Hunting permits can be arranged by the local hotels, though it is perhaps wise to have this organised in advance, perhaps by a tour company. The season runs from December to February.

Around Tunis

Getting Your Bearings

The Tunis of today tells a tale of two cities. The first is the old fortified *médina* (old city), filled with mosques and markets and all the atmosphere and traditions of an old North African town; the second, the consciously planned Ville Nouvelle, the new city that emerged in the 19th century and grew apace with the French as the colonial power.

The capital is by far the largest of Tunisia's towns with about a fifth of the country's population. Situated near the shores of Lake Tunis on a raised spit of land, Tunis offers visitors a glimpse of history and a taste of Arabic culture alongside the comforts and designs of a modern age such as the attractive art nouveau buildings that enhance the city. But there has also been a conscious effort to adapt, with a keen interest in coolness, shade and air represented by balconies, terraces, awnings and ubiquitous whitewashing.

A channel connects the port basin at Tunis with the sea around 10km away at La Goulette (Halq al-Wadi), and there is a causeway across the lake as well. Very close to Tunis lies historic and attractive Carthage, as well as the famous hilltop village of Sidi Bou Saïd and the seaside resorts of La Marsa and Gammarth.

Previous page: Crudely fashioned soldier puppets on sale in Sidi Bou Saïd

Above: An excavated stone head in Carthage

Cap Gammarth

Ariana

8

Soukra

9 Gammarth

8 La Marsa

4 Sidi Bou Saïd

5 Jemaa ez Zitouna

3 Carthage

Musée du Bardo
6

2 Ville Nouvelle

1 The Médina

7 La Goulette

Manougla

Golfe de Tunis

0   10 km

0   5 miles

1

Mornag

Mohammedia

The busy
marina at Sidi
Bou Saïd

Enter the charming world of the Médina, traverse the boulevards of Ville Nouvelle, dig into the ancient treasures of Carthage and visit the seaside resorts near by.

Around Tunis in Three Days

Day One

Morning

Stroll around the **⓪ Médina** (➤ 50) and take in the sights and smells of this medieval maze. Visit the Great Mosque or **⑤ Jemaa ez Zitouna** (➤ 60) and three nearby *madrassas* (below), centres of Islamic studies.

Explore the fascinating *souqs* (markets). The intricate mixture of charming sights – shops filled with perfumes, gold, carpets, ceramics and spices – should leave you with an appetite and certainly a thirst.

Try a chic restaurant like Dar el-Jeld (➤ 65), in the heart of the Médina for a luxurious introduction to Tunisian cuisine.

Afternoon

Staying within the Médina, you can walk easily to the three main buildings in the southern part of the old town: these will give you a good idea of the splendid local architecture (right); the Tourbet el-Bey, or royal tombs (➤ 52), and the two classical houses, Dar Ben Abdallah and **Dar Othman** (➤ 51).

Evening

After an action-packed day of sightseeing, why not visit a Tunisian cabaret show? Try Chez Gaston (➤ 66) on the rue de Yougoslavie.

Day Two

Morning

Head for the **2 Ville Nouvelle** (➤ 54).
Enjoy the 1km walk down the
"Champs Élysées of Tunis" and then
make for the Parc de Belvedere, which
offers views of the city and often
enjoys cool breezes. There's a pleasant café in the park where you can
enjoy a light lunch.

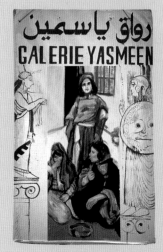

Afternoon

Take a taxi to the **6 Musée du Bardo**
(➤ 60). Get ready for a feast of art,
excavations, mosaics and Tunisian history.

Evening

Head back to avenue Habib Bourguiba
and the El Hana International (➤ 63).
The top floor of the hotel is perfect for sunset views
all over the city. The Café des Deux Avenues on the
promenade is a delightful spot for dinner and people-watching. Finish the night dancing at the
hotel's own nightclub, Le Jocker.

Day Three

Morning

Take the TGM Métro out to **3 Carthage** (➤ 56).
If you arrive early enough you should have time
to visit almost all the ruins of this once mighty
city. However, the Byrsa Hill area, the theatre,
the ancient baths and the sinister Tophet will
satisfy most.

Afternoon

If you have spent hours rummaging around
the ruins then you'll certainly be ready
for lunch. Head out to **4 Sidi Bou Saïd**
(above, ➤ 58) and dine at the Café des
Nattes. Explore the hilltop village of
Sidi Bou Saïd with its lovely views.
Visit the palace of the Baron
d'Erlanger, Ennejma Ezzahra.

Evening

For dinner try the Hotel Sidi
Bou Saïd (➤ 64). You can
relax with drinks on the terrace overlooking the sea at
sunset and dine upstairs.
There are often cabaret shows
on as well.

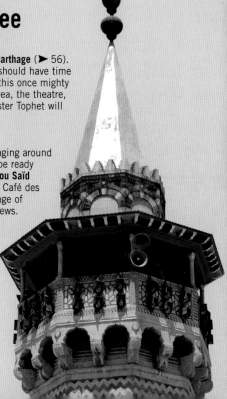

❶ The Médina

Clustered within the *médina* (old city) are most of the interesting buildings of Tunis. This 1km sq area is a UNESCO World Heritage Site, and is home to many mosques and intriguing covered *souqs* (markets) over-flowing with spices and cloth, perfumes and brassware, all in a maze of narrow, twisting streets.

You can enter the *médina* by the Bab el-Bahr, the Sea Gate on the east, where an arched gateway was built in 1848. Although the walls have long gone, the gate stands at the end of the arcaded avenue de France in the place de la Victoire. Here you abandon the European-style boulevards and enter a maze. The sinuous rue de la Kasbah leads into the heart of the *médina* where you can stop and admire the **Mosquée de Hammoudda Pacha** – named after an Italian who converted

The Bab el-Bahr or Sea Gate in the place de la Victoire

to Islam – which is notable for its charming Turkish minaret built in 1655. Just further along rue de la Kasbah is the west gate to the *médina*, where the **Dar el-Bey**, the Prime Minister's office sits on the place du Gouvernement. This is a very attractive square with elegant fountains and Moorish-style government offices. To the south, you find yourself in the heart of the markets, delightful covered areas originally built in the 13th and 14th centuries by Hafsid rulers. Vibrant colours, elaborately decorated shops and opulent displays of tempting goods are the keynotes here.

Near by is the 17th-century mosque of **Sidi Yusuf**, which has an octagonal minaret, the oldest of this type in Tunis. Returning parallel to Mosquée de Hammoudda Pacha you'll come across the Bibliothèque Nationale (National Library) which was in fact a former Turkish army barracks. Flanking the library is the most significant landmark within Tunis, **Jemaa ez Zitouna** (➤ 60).

Dar Othman

Turning south by Jemaa ez Zitouna, near the minaret of the Jemaa el-Jadid (the New Mosque) you come to the Dar Othman, residence of Othman, *dey* (governor) of Tunis from 1598 to 1610. The palace is a splendid example of Tunisian architecture, built around a court planted with cypress, hibiscus and lemon trees. Behind a marble façade

A perfume seller surrounded by his merchandise

an entrance of elaborately decorated tiles leads to a court with a garden, opening out towards four T-shaped rooms, each richly adorned with mosaics and beautiful pierced plaster-work. Nowadays Dar Othman houses the Conservation de la Médina offices which work to preserve the monuments and splendour of the old city.

The entrance to one of Tunis' many *hammams* or Turkish bath-houses

In the rue des Libraires are three old **madrassas**, (teaching schools for Islam) – du Palmier, Bachiya and Slimaniya – dating from the 18th century. *Madrassas* are essentially universities but visitors are welcome. The grand architecture of these three schools is an education in itself.

If men wish to try a traditional "Turkish bath", the **Hammam Kachachine** is opposite the Medersa Slimaniya. *Hammam* is a strong tradition in Tunisia, dating back to Roman times. Visitors are provided with changing rooms and towels, and can relax for an hour or two with hot baths, cold baths and hot rooms before emerging scrubbed and shiny back in the *médina* again.

In the south of the old *médina* there are several interesting places to visit. The **Tourbet el-Bey** is the lavish mausoleum of the Husaynid rulers. Between the mausoleum and the Dar Othman is the **Mosquée des Teinturiers** (Mosque of the Dye-

makers). Just south of this is the **Musée des Arts Populaires et Traditions** (Museum of Popular Arts and Traditions). Previously known as Dar Ben Abdallah, this impressively grand house dates from the 18th century. Displays and objets d'art are housed around a cool, marble-paved courtyard.

Brassware for sale outside a shop on the rue Jemaa ez Zitouna

TAKING A BREAK

The **Café M'rabet** (or "*Marabout*") in the Souq et Trok (➤ 65) in the *médina* is a pleasant and cool place to stop for a rest, recovering with a glass of mint tea (or a water pipe). The upstairs restaurant has a splendid view of Jemaa ez Zitouna.

Dar Othman
➕ 178 C1
✉ rue Sidi Kacem, Médina
🕐 Mon–Sat 9:30–4:30
🎟 Free

Hammam Kachachine
➕ 178 C2
✉ rue de Libraries, Médina
🕐 Daily 5–5 🎟 Inexpensive

Musée des Arts Populaires et Traditions
➕ 178 C1
✉ rue Sidi Kacem, Médina
☎ 01 256915
🕐 Tue–Sun 9:30–4:30
🎟 Inexpensive

THE MÉDINA: INSIDE INFO

Top tip If you intend to visit mosques or *madrassas* **dress respectfully**. Shorts, vests, short skirts and the like are simply unacceptable. Visitors must take off their shoes when entering the interior of the mosque. Activities such as photography should be avoided during formal prayer times.

Hidden gem Seek out the exotic and beautifully decorated **perfume shops** in the Souq el Attarine, near Jemaa ez Zitouna. This was the place of honour for what was once considered the noblest trade of all. You can try out samples of the rich array of oriental scents and perhaps buy some small phials as souvenirs.

2 Ville Nouvelle

The layout of the new city is based around the "Champs Elysées" of Tunis, the wide, tree-shaded avenue Habib Bourguiba.

Starting at the avenue de France by the main gate to the *médina*, the 1km-long avenue Habib Bourguiba passes the place de l'Indépendance with its statue of famous Tunisian writer, Ibn Khaldun (1332–95), and heads east to the port. This European-style avenue forms the centrepiece for a rectangular grid of boulevards.

You will find a stroll in the new town worthwhile both for the pleasant colonial architecture and the atmosphere. Just outside the *médina* to the east, on the avenue, is the **Cathédrale de St Vincent de Paul**, built in 1882. There are two flanking towers topped with domes similar to that of Sacré Coeur in Paris, and a rather bizarre figure of God the Father whose head and hands project out high over the portico. The church still functions, with Masses every day and twice on Sundays. Across the road sits the French Embassy, built in 1862, which was once the heart of Tunisian government.

At No 50 on avenue Habib Bourguiba you will find fashionable and popular meeting places in the cafés and bars of the tall blue hotel Africa El Mouradi (➤ 63). There is also the imposing white façade of the **Théâtre Municipal**, with its art nouveau-style decoration around the doorways and gratuitous little round corner balconies. Near by is the elegant Carlton hotel (➤ 63), built in 1926 with white columns and arched façades. In the side streets are numerous restaurants. Just ahead at the open-work clock tower of place du 7 Novembre with its display of fountains is another intersection. The Tourism Office is at this junction (avenue Mohammed V), and beyond is the strange inverted pyramid shape of the now closed Grand Hotel du Lac. By the port at the end of the avenue is the station for the TGM to Carthage and Sidi Bou Saïd, and the Métro around the city.

The façade of the Catholic Cathédrale de St Vincent de Paul

The old
French-built
Théâtre
Municipal on
avenue Habib
Bourguiba

Parc de Belvedere

A little over 1km to the north of avenue Habib Bourguiba lies
the Parc de Belvedere. Built for the pleasure and relaxation of
the French residents, the park is named after its charming
18th-century *qubba*, or domed belvedere. Situated on a hilltop, you can catch the cool sea breezes and escape the heat
and hustle of the city. There is also a little zoo, a café on an
island in the lake, a large fountain and a good view of Tunis
from the top of the hill. To get here take bus No 5 from
avenue Habib Bourguiba.

TAKING A BREAK

Avenue Habib Bourguiba is dotted with pleasant pavement
cafés such as the **Panorama Café** and the **Brasserie des
Deux Avenues** opposite the theatre, where you can relax
under a parasol with a drink at any time of the day. In the
evening it is particularly lively when the working day is over
andmusicians entertain.

**Cathédrale de St Vincent
de Paul**
✚ 179 D3
✉ avenue Habib Bourguiba
◷ All day 🎟 Free

Parc de Belvedere
✚ 181 D3
✉ avenue Taieb Mehiri
◷ Zoo open: Tue–Sun 10–4
🎟 Inexpensive

VILLE NOUVELLE: INSIDE INFO

Top tip Try one of the many **pâtisseries** along avenue Habib Bourguiba; they all
have huge selections of croissants, baguettes, crêpes and cakes.

❸ Carthage

Imagination is almost all we have to go on to envisage Carthage in all its splendour. Once the largest city in Africa, it was first settled by the Phoenicians, then conquered by the Romans who built theatres, baths and an arena for gladiators. Nowadays it is a lush suburb of Tunis, but you can still explore the ruins and visit the museums which record the long and proud history of this once great capital of the ancient world.

Byrsa Hill

A picturesque place to begin is Byrsa Hill, with its magnificent panorama over the lake and the bay. Here was the Carthaginian citadel, the temple of Eshmun, a market, council hall and other temples. On the Byrsa, the Romans built their forum, as well as a temple dedicated to the gods Jupiter, Juno and Minerva, and another to Aesculapius, the god of medicine, containing sculptures, a basilica and a library. The ruins can be seen today in front of the museum, the **Musée National de Carthage** (National Museum of Carthage) which was formerly a convent. The museum has wisely separated the excavations, treasures and displays into three sections: Punic (Phoenician), Roman and Christian. The ruins of some buildings dating back to the 4th century BC can still be seen in the garden of the museum. Just behind the museum sits the **Cathédrale de St-Louis** which is now a culture centre.

A section of the huge Antonine Baths, the largest outside Rome

Thermes d'Antonin Pius

Back down on the waterfront you should pay a visit to the Thermes d'Antonin Pius (Antonine Baths) which is probably the best-preserved and most spectacular site in Carthage. Built by the Romans in the 2nd century AD, these baths were second only to the great baths in Rome. The ruins can be observed from a viewing platform.

Other Sites Worth Seeing

From the Byrsa, inland to the west, lie the **hippodrome**, the **amphitheatre**, and the **Citernes de la Malga** (Malga Cisterns), where the water arriving from Zaghwan via an aqueduct was stored. The ruined baths of **Gargilius**, an archaeological park of Roman villas and the **Théâtre d'Hadrian** (Theatre of Hadrian) stand to the north. To the south of the old port stretches a tranquil garden known as the **Tophet** which hides a dark past. It was at this mystic Phoenician sanctuary that thousands of children were sacrificed to the Punic gods.

A 3rd-century mosaic depicting a satyr on display in the Musée National de Carthage

TAKING A BREAK

Near the ancient ports in the rue Hannibal is a cosy, up-market restaurant called **Le Punique** (➤ 64) which offers an international menu.

➕ 181 D3
✉ 16km east of Tunis
🚊 TGM every 20 mins, stopping in Carthage at Salammbô, Byrsa, Dermech and Hannibal

Musée National de Carthage
✉ Byrsa Hill
☎ 01 730036
🕐 Tue–Sun 8–7 (8:30–5:30 in winter)
🚊 TGM Carthage–Hannibal

Thermes d'Antonin Pius
✉ avenue des Thermes d'Antonin
🕐 Tue–Sun 8–7 (8:30–5:30 in winter
🚊 TGM Carthage–Hannibal

CARTHAGE: INSIDE INFO

Top tips Carthage can be reached on the **TGM Tunis Marine** train. It's only a 30-minute journey and the last train back to Tunis leaves just after midnight.

• If you don't have a car, arrange with **one taxi driver** to take you to all the different sites. This is much cheaper and more efficient than trying to do it step by step.

• Check at the TGM station or at the entrance to Byrsa Hill for an **all-inclusive Carthage ticket**. This should cover fees to all sites and could easily save you some money.

4 Sidi Bou Saïd

With its brilliantly whitewashed houses, Sidi Bou Saïd has the distinctive air of a small Greek island village. The beautiful upper section of the town, with its steep-stepped streets, offers stunning views out to sea, and the dwellings below are surrounded by bougainvillaea and palm trees. This hilltop village northeast of Tunis has had an unusual history due to an exceptional foreigner who visited the town in the 13th century.

Arriving in the lower village, you might wonder what all the fuss is about. But when you climb up, or approach from Carthage or La Marsa past the president's palace on the road to the top of the village, it becomes obvious why this village is so well known. The views are ever more stunning.

The older history of the village is fairly conventional. A 10th-century *ribat* or fortified monastery was constructed here by Arabs. The views over the sea from both sides of the headland make its defensive position obvious. A 13th-century Sufi (holy man) from Morocco named Sidi Bou Saïd (in unabbreviated Arabic, *Sayyid Abu Said Kalafa ibn Yahya al-Temimi al-Beji*) stopped here on his way back from the pilgrimage to Mecca. He was believed to be able to cure poisonous scorpion bites and rheumatism. A community developed around the *zaouia* (tomb) where he was buried. Nowadays, a festival commemorates him each year in August.

By the 19th century, as colonial expatriates began to seek tranquillity and lovely views, French-owned villas were built, culminating in 1912–22 with the cliff-side palace and gardens called **Ennejma Ezzahra**, built by Baron Rodolphe d'Erlanger, an Englishman who hailed from a prosperous French banking family. The baron obtained a ruling that the only colours that could be used to paint the outside of houses were blue and white. His own villa now houses the **Centre des Musiques Arabes et Méditerranéennes** (Centre

A woman walking along a cobbled street beneath attractive, blue-painted window grilles

for Arab and Mediterranean Music), with a wonderful museum of Arab musical instruments, paintings and a private *hammam* (Turkish bath).

Sidi Bou Saïd is undeniably beautiful. Artists such as Paul Klee and Louis Moillet came here and painted, inspired by the clarity of the air and the vibrant colours.

A view of the main coast road from the Café Sidi Chabaane

TAKING A BREAK

In front of the mosque on place Sidi Bou Saïd is the ever popular **Café des Nattes**, which is a perfect spot for a coffee or a cup of mint tea and where you can sit and even catch a glimpse of the sea. The **Café Sidi Chabaane** on the outskirts of town is expensive but luxurious and offers majestic views over the marina and the Gulf of Tunis.

🚩 181 D3	**Centre des Musiques Arabes et**
✉ 20km northeast of Tunis	**Mediterranéennes**
🚇 TGM from Tunis every 20 mins	✉ Ennejma Ezzahra 🕐 Tue–Sun 9–12, 2–7, (2–5 only in winter) 🎫 Inexpensive

SIDI BOU SAÏD: INSIDE INFO

Top tip Sidi Bou Saïd is **easily reached by TGM Métro** which leaves from avenue de Habib Bourguiba in Tunis every 20 minutes. The journey takes 35 minutes and the last train back is at midnight.

Hidden gem There is a tranquil **Muslim cemetery** on top of the hill above town which is a serene spot to take in some wonderful views of the sea and the town.

At Your Leisure

⑤ Jemaa ez Zitouna

The greatest mosque in all Tunis (though smaller than the Grande Mosquée de Sidi Oqba in Kairouan) is in the centre of the *médina* (➤ 50) – the Mosque of the Olive Tree, the Great Mosque or Jemaa ez Zitouna. All mosques with the exception of the Zitouna are open to non-Muslims who can survey the Zitouna from a viewing enclosure overlooking the vast courtyard. Its history, as usual, has been one of alterations and enlargements, but its beginning was in the 9th century, when stone plundered from the ruins of Roman Carthage was brought to Tunis to build its outer wall. The mosque became an important Islamic study centre in the 13th and 14th centuries, and has continued to be so except for an interval during the presidency of Habib Bourguiba, who was anxious to reduce militant Islam in the country. The mosque houses a very old library, with one of the greatest collections of Arabic books in the world.

🚏 178 C2 ✉ rue Jemaa ez Zitouna, Médina 🕔 Sat–Thu 8 am–noon (closed Muslim holidays) 💵 Inexpensive

A bust of the Emperor Lucius Verus on display in the Bardo Museum

⑥ Musée du Bardo

The Musée du Bardo (Bardo Museum) is one of the world's great museums, principally because of its unique speciality, the mosaics of Roman Tunisia.

The museum is a former country palace of the Husaynid rulers, a grand setting for the glories of ancient Tunisia, with its Moorish architecture, including wonderfully complicated domes, ceilings, balconies, plasterwork and tiling. The collection covers the gamut of Tunisian history, from Stone Age to Carthaginian, Roman, Christian and Islamic eras. There is impressive Carthaginian terracotta, and a wealth of Roman sculpture, glassware and vases.

The star attractions are the Roman mosaics (➤ 30). Most spectacular is perhaps the *Triumph of Neptune*, a huge composition depicting sea creatures. It occupies the entire floor of a splendid domed room. In the Dougga Room is a further Neptune composition, of the 2nd century, with the god riding forward in his *quadriga* or four-horse sea chariot. Another charming Dougga mosaic shows a tale from the *Odyssey*, in which Ulysses, desiring to hear the song of the terrible bird-footed Sirens, has himself bound to the mast of his ship as his men, ears blocked against the wonderful sound, row past unmoved.

➕ 181 D3 ✉ Route de Bizerte, quartier Bardo ☎ 71 513842 🕐 Tue–Sun 8:30–5:30 (9:30–4:30 in winter) 🚇 Métro Léger Line 4 💰 Moderate

7 La Goulette

This is the exit point of the Tunis–Mediterranean canal; its Arabic name is Halq al-Wadi, *halq* meaning throat, just as *goulette* means "gullet". Its situation on a sandbar 11km from Tunis has established La Goulette as a popular resort and residential suburb, attractive for its beach and fish restaurants. In the past it was a famous pirate haunt (▶ 12) and you can see the remains of a *kasbah* or fortress which was built at the time of the Spanish conquest of Tunis in 1535.

➕ 181 D3 ✉ 15km northeast of Tunis 🚇 TGM Tunis Marine

8 La Marsa

La Marsa, north of Tunis, is a popular and prosperous suburb. It has a Côte d'Azur flavour with its cliffside roads lined with palm trees, and a long, sandy beach. The blue-and-white-painted Ksar Esaada, a former palace, was at one time the home of Habib Bourguiba, and is now the town hall. As with Gammarth, the beach is inevitably crowded in summer and at weekends as Tunis residents escape to the seaside.

➕ 181 D4 ✉ 16km northeast of Tunis 🚇 TGM Tunis Marine

9 Gammarth

The once simple fishing village of Gammarth has now become a major resort, just a few kilometres further north from La Marsa and with plenty of up-market hotels and restaurants. The sandy beach near by at Raoued Plage is also very popular. The Roman historian Pliny (AD 61–113) considered the Tunisian coastline one of the finest, and modern taste seems to agree with him, to the great benefit of Tunisia's burgeoning tourist trade and economy.

➕ 181 D4 ✉ 20km northeast of Tunis 🚌 20B from Jardin Thameur, Tunis

A finely decorated door leading to the Bardo Museum

Where to... Stay

Prices
Expect to pay for a standard double room per night
£ under TD50   ££ TD50–TD100   £££ over TD100

Tunis has a variety of hotels to suit all tastes. Most of the best accommodation is found in the Ville Nouvelle. There are, sadly, no hotels of any quality in the old *médina*. Sidi Bou Said is quieter than Tunis, but also has a number of good places to stay.

CARTHAGE

Palm Beach Reine Didon ££

Among the relatively few hotels in the largely residential quarter of Carthage, the Reine Didon is the top hotel. Situated near the Carthage Hannibal TGM station, its chief distinction is the views over the sea from its clean, quiet rooms, and its ideal setting for exploring the ruins of the old Punic and Roman city.

➕ 181 D3 ☒ rue Mendès-France, Byrsa Hill ☎ 71 733433; fax: 71 732599

GAMMARTH

Abou Nawas Gammarth £££

A lovely setting on the northern part of the Bay of Tunis, the Abou Nawas is well situated for the airport. An incredible array of facilities includes four restaurants, a nightclub, tennis courts, sauna and massage rooms. Accommodation ranges from apartments to deluxe villas.

➕ 181 D4 ☒ avenue Taïeb Mehiri ☎ 71 741444; fax: 71 740400; email: gammarth@abounawas.com.tn

SIDI BOU SAÏD

Dar Saïd ££

Sidi Bou Saïd is well served for hotels, but Dar Saïd is the most charming, as well as the priciest of those in the village. The hotel has been beautifully refurbished, preserving its traditional architectural features. Perched high above the village, with a garden terrace view of the 576m-high peak of Bou Kurnine on the north coast, the building is elegant, with lovely tile work, and its very own *hammam* or Turkish bath. Other facilities include a pretty sitting room, a charming tiny fountain court, and a swimming pool and bar with views over the Mediterranean Sea, shaded by orange trees often laden with fruit. There are nightly shows featuring live traditional Tunisian music, a dancing girl in an elaborate costume, and a man who cleverly balances incredible numbers of pots on his head. All rooms are air-conditioned with satellite television and a mini-bar. An elegant restaurant serves French, Tunisian and international cuisine.

➕ 181 D3 ☒ rue Toumi ☎ 71 729666; fax: 71 729599; www.darsaid.com.tn

Sidi Bou Farès £

Quite different from the opulence of Dar Saïd, Sidi Bou Farès is a pleasant hotel in the centre of the old village, near the Café des Nattes. An entrance opening directly off a narrow sloping street leads into a vestibule, and then into a charming courtyard around which the rooms are arranged. The rooms are vaulted cells, white painted or with zigzag brick roofs, some with an attached bathroom, some just with washing facilities, and shared toilets and showers elsewhere. Furnishings are simple. The atmosphere is very pleasant, with a shady fig tree and other plants in the courtyard, and scattered chairs and tables where you can take your breakfast.

➕ 181 D3 ✉ 15 rue Sidi Bou Farès, central Sidi Bou Saïd ☎ 71 740091; fax: 71 728868; email: hotel.boufares@gnet.tn

Sidi Bou Saïd £££

Owned by the Tunisian National Tourist Office this small hotel is a modern structure set alone on a hill with wonderful views over Carthage and Gammarth, and also the sea. The very pleasant double rooms, all with balconies, are air-conditioned. Amenities include a swimming pool, tennis courts, bar and popular restaurant. There is sometimes a special evening with a regional cabaret show in the restaurant featuring a traditional Tunisian band, dancing and feats of pot-balancing.

➕ 181 D3 ✉ avenue Sidi Dhrif, Gammarth, just over the hill from the presidential palace and Sidi Bou Saïd ☎ 71 740411; fax: 71 745129

Africa El Mouradi £££

In a large blue tower opposite the El Hana International Hotel, the old Africa Hotel, now part of the El Mouradi hotel chain, is a first-class hotel. It has a pleasant spacious foyer with a bar and first-floor restaurant offering buffet lunches. There are splendid views over the town and the Lake of Tunis from most of its rooms. Facilities include a cinema, large pool and business centre.

➕ 179 F3 ✉ 50 avenue Habib Bourguiba ☎ 71 347477; fax: 71 347432; www.elmouradi.com

Carlton ££

The Carlton, noted for its excellent service, is centrally located on the main street of the Ville Nouvelle, just down the road from the huge El Hana International. It's an elegant building with an attractive, old colonial-style facade. The well-designed rooms are comfortable,

but those at the front can be a little noisy. The hotel's ground floor contains a shopping mall with over 20 boutiques.

➕ 179 F3 ✉ 31 avenue Habib Bourguiba ☎ 71 330644; fax: 71 338168; email: carlton@planet.tn

El Hana International ££

The El Hana, in the centre of the town, is a vast first-class hotel of rather soulless modern architecture, occupying a large block on Tunis' main avenue. The café des Deux Avenues on the ground floor opens to the street, and is a very popular meeting place. There is also a rooftop bar with excellent views over the entire city.

➕ 179 E3 ✉ 49 avenue Habib Bourguiba ☎ 71 331144; fax: 71 349071; www.elhana.com

La Maison Dorée £

A great value choice near Tunis' main thoroughfare avenue Habib Bourguiba, and not far from the main market and the railway sta-

tion. It is still immaculately maintained by the French colonial founder's family, with rooms clean and well kept. The 1950s-era furniture gives the place character. Rooms at the back are quieter, while the front rooms can be noisy due to the regular trams running passed the hotel.

➕ 179 E2 ✉ 6 rue de Hollande, entry on 3 rue el-Koufa ☎ 71 240631; fax: 71 332401

Majestic ££

One of the few remaining turn-of-the-20th-century hotels left in Tunis, the Majestic retains an aura of days gone by. The big terrace on the first floor provides an excellent vantage point for viewing the busy avenue de Paris. The rooms are large and spotlessly clean. There's a good restaurant serving French, Tunisian and international cuisines, and there's also a comfortable bar.

➕ 179 E4 ✉ 36 avenue de Paris ☎ 71 332666; fax: 71 336908; email: majestic@gnet.tn

Where to...
Eat and Drink

Prices

Expect to pay per person for a standard three-course meal, excluding drinks and service charges

£ under TD15   **££** TD15–TD30   **£££** over TD30

CARTHAGE

L'Odyssée £

L'Odyssée has a pleasant terrace that overlooks the beach in the Salammbô quarter of the town. The restaurant serves good-value meals that include a delicious Berber-style oven baked lamb with herbs.

➕ 181 D3 ⬛ Salammbô Beach ☎ 71 720911 ⓒ Daily 11–2.30, 6–10:30

Le Punique £££

Situated near the ancient ports in Carthage's rue Hannibal, Le Punique specialises in Moroccan dishes. It offers an up-market, cosy restaurant in a suburb of comfortable villas.

➕ 181 D3 ⬛ Hotel-Résidence de Carthage, 16 rue Hannibal, Salammbô ☎ 71 731072 ⓒ Mon–Sat 11–3, 6–11

LA MARSA

Café Saf Saf £

This is a very popular spot in summertime, with terraces for taking tea or eating a light meal. The café serves pâtisserie, some delicious Tunisian snacks, soups and the like.

In the middle of the café a tethered camel labours around an old well.

➕ 181 D4 ⬛ place Saf Saf ⓒ Daily 10–10 (summer only)

La Falaise £££

The town of La Marsa, has many restaurants and cafes; La Falaise is one of the very best. As the road begins climbing towards Sidi Bou Saïd you'll see this delightful restaurant on the left side. Here you can experience a variety of Tunisian and international cuisine. A superb fish *couscous* is among the recommended dishes.

➕ 181 D4 ⬛ rue Sidi Dhrif, La Marsa Corniche ☎ 71 747806 ⓒ Daily 11–2:30, 6–11

SIDI BOU SAÏD

Le Chergui £

This popular restaurant is situated just below the mosque in the centre of Sidi Bou Saïd, a very agreeable location for an inexpensive lunch or dinner. With its open-air terrace and bench seats covered with local carpets it makes an attractive show, and has a good view over the sea. The barbecued lamb is excellent.

➕ 181 D3 ⬛ 39 avenue Habib Thameur ☎ 71 740987 ⓒ Daily 11 am–11 pm

Sidi Bou Saïd ££

This hotel restaurant, situated up the hill on the Gammarth side of Sidi Bou Saïd, serves a fine mix of Tunisian and international food. The special presentations of regional cuisine, some of which are delicious, and the lights of Gammarth glittering below, make a very pleasant and interesting evening. Try some of the Kasserine desserts such as *rfissa* (sweet couscous) or the unusual dish of *samsa zgougou* (sweet pudding of ground pine leaves).

➕ 181 D3 ⬛ Hotel Sidi Bou Saïd, avenue Sidi Dhrif, Gammarth, just over the hill from the presidential palace and Sidi Bou Saïd ☎ 71 740411 ⓒ Daily 11–2, 5–10:30

Where to... Shop

TUNIS

Café M'rabet £-££

A wonderful old Ottoman café on the ground floor with a restaurant upstairs serving a number of different set meals. In the evenings, for a small extra charge, traditional Berber music and dance performances are staged. The mint tea and water pipes are worth trying

🚹 178 B2 ⊠ Souq et Trouk, Médina
☎ 71 261729 ⊗ Daily 10 am–11 pm

Capitole ££

A plain but pleasant compromise in the central Ville Nouvelle is the relatively humble Capitole. Here, among many other very good dishes, you can try a vast *couscous royale* or a Tunisian *brik* with tuna. Like so many Tunisian restaurants, outside the *zones touristiques*, there is no alcohol served.

🚹 179 F3 ⊠ 60 avenue Habib Bourguiba, almost opposite the El Hana Hotel ☎ 71 256601 ⊗ Daily 10:30–2, 5:30–11

Chez Nous ££

An old-fashioned Tunis restaurant rather living on its reputation, nevertheless it still offers a fine *à la carte* menu. The food is mainly French, with few Tunisian specialities. The walls are lined with black and white photographs of the Chez Nous' many famous guests including Muhammad Ali and Edith Piaf. Alcohol is served.

🚹 179 E3 ⊠ 5 rue de Marseille
☎ 71 243048 ⊗ Mon–Sat 11–2, 6–11; closed Ramadan

Dar el-Jeld £££

Top of the range for dining in style, the Dar el-Jeld, in the heart of the *médina*, is housed in an elegantly restored Tunis mansion. It's expensive, but the excellent traditional Tunisian cuisine is worth the outlay. You can dine to the sound of the lute amid comfortable furnishings.

🚹 178 B3 ⊠ 5 rue Dar el-Jeld ☎ 71 560916; www.dareljeld.tourism.tn
⊗ Mon–Sat 11–2:30, 5:30–11; closed August and Ramadan

Rue Jemaa ez Zitouna, which runs from the Bab el-Bahr through the heart of the Tunis *médina* to the central *souqs*, is jam-packed with shops selling every sort of souvenir from the tasteless to the sophisticated. There's a lot of kitsch – Tunisia probably has more stuffed camels of all sizes than any country on earth – but there's also a fine selection of rugs and carpets, pottery and ceramics, copper, brass, leather goods and jewellery. Beyond the rue Jemaa ez Zitouna there are plenty more souvenir and handicraft shops on the rue de la Kasbah, as well as in the *souqs* themselves.

Within this maze of shopping streets, rue **Jemaa ez Zitouna** is the best place to find silk-screened T-shirts with appropriately Tunisian motifs, as well as items such as Tunisian *jellaba* robes, traditional *chechia* hats, *babouche* slippers and *chicha* water pipes.

The Tunis *souqs* have changed little over the centuries, and many are specific to a particular trade. The **Souq el-Attarine**, for example, is the place to go for perfumes, while the **Souq el-Kababjia** specialises in silks and the **Souq du Cuivre** in brass and copperware.

Shopping in the Tunis *médina*, and especially in the *souqs*, involves bargaining as a matter of course (▶ 42), but for many visitors this is all part of the fun. If, on the other hand, you prefer not to bargain, then your best bet is to visit Société de Commercialisation des Produits de l'Artisanats (generally shortened to **SOCOPA**, tel: 71 793366) on the corner of avenue Carthage and avenue Habib Bourguiba. This large department

Where to...
Be Entertained

CABARET AND NIGHTCLUBS

For evening dining and entertainment Tunis has a number of restaurants that offer cabaret, folk music and dance, as you eat. Among them are **Chez Gaston** at 73, rue de Yougoslavie (tel: 71 340417), **El Mazar**, above the La Mamma restaurant, rue de Marseilles (tel: 71 241256), and **M'rabet** at Souq El Trouk in the *médina*, above the Café M'rabet (▶ 65). The latter sometimes features a belly dancer, which is fairly risqué for Tunis. At Sidi Bou Saïd the **Hotel Sidi Bou Saïd** (▶ 63), about 1km north of town on the La Marsa road, hosts special evenings with a regional show. This involves a small orchestra in costume, with pipes and drums, accompanied by local dancing and pot-balancing displays.

Nightclubs in some of the better Tunis hotels include the **Club 2001** in the Hotel Abou Nouwas El Mechtel, Belvedere Park, avenue Ouled Haffouz (tel: 71 783200), **Le Jocker** in the El Hana International Hotel on avenue Habib Bourguiba (▶ 63), and **Club Sheherezade** in the Hotel Abou Nawas at Park Kennedy, avenue Mohammed V (tel: 71 350355).

CINEMAS

Tunis has plenty of cinemas showing popular Arab blockbusters and the latest Hollywood hits, though these are most likely to be dubbed into French. Two of the best are **Le Capitole**, next to the Café de Paris on avenue Habib Bourguiba, and **La Parnasse** in the up-market shopping arcade between rue d'Alger and rue Ali Bach Hamba, just off avenue Habib Bourguiba.

BARS

Most bars in Tunis are unlikely to appeal to visitors, especially women. Many would feel more comfortable in their hotel's bar, though the **Bar Coquille** beside the Restaurant Carcassonne on avenue de Carthage is appealing for a drink.

THEATRES AND FESTIVALS

The **Municipal theatre** on avenue Habib Bourguiba is used for concerts. The programme for this and other similar performances and local festivals is available at the Tourism Office. At Sidi Bou Saïd the house of the late Baron d'Erlanger, now the **Centre des Musiques Arabes et Mediterranéennes** (▶ 58), stages regular concerts.

store has a comprehensive collection of handicrafts from all over the country, all clearly marked with fixed prices. The upside is that shopping for presents and souvenirs is very easy here, but the downside is that everything is rather more expensive than in the souqs – especially if you bargain hard.

Other, similar fixed-price outlets are provided by the Offices Nationales del'Artisanat Tunisien (ONAT), represented in Tunis by the **Magazin Mohammed V** on avenue Mohammed V (tel: 71 346479), and **Magazin Den-Den** (particularly good for rugs and carpets) on the place de l'Independance (tel: 71 512400).

Also highly recommended is **Mains des Femmes** ("women's hands") on the first floor above the Banque de l'Habitat at 47 avenue Habib Bourguiba (tel: 71 330789, open Mon–Sat, 9:30–1, 3–6:30). Here you will find a good selection of jewellery, Tunisian dolls and wooden toys, as well as embroidery.

The North

Getting Your Bearings

The northern part of Tunisia is a true delight to travel in. The region has an excellent climate and splendid views along the northern Tunisian seacoast and among the inland hills and forests. The main towns are the large port of Bizerte to the east and the resort of Tabarka in the west. Both are historic places that have experienced the full effect of events in Tunisia from Carthaginian times to the present, and contain castles and other buildings that are worth exploring. Not far from Bizerte and the ruins of the once important Carthaginian–Roman city of Utica are several charming beaches.

The town of Tabarka can be used as a centre for visiting the northwestern region. The cork oak forests around Aïn Draham are definitely worth a visit, and perhaps Béja, a modest inland market town situated on the Majarda, the only substantial river in the country. It is also not far from Tabarka to one of the most important Roman sites of Tunisia, Bulla Regia, an ancient capital of the Numidian kings. The site is especially fascinating for its well-preserved underground Roman villas.

Previous page: Colourful fishing boats moored in the sheltered harbour at Bizerte
Left: A statue of former President Habib Bourguiba and his dog in the centre of Tabarka

Aïn Ker

51

Nefza

2 Tabarka

Fatnassa

▲
805m

697m
▲

○ Babouch

8 Aïn Draham

Béja 10

17

11

Hammam Saïala ○

627m
▲

○ Bou Salem   75E

76

9
Chemtou
and Thuburnica

3 Bulla Regia

75

○ Jendouba

○ Meskine

★ Don't Miss

At Your Leisure

An unusual monument in Béja to the
storks that nest locally

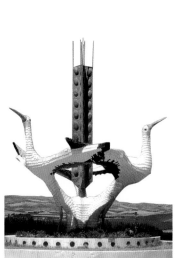

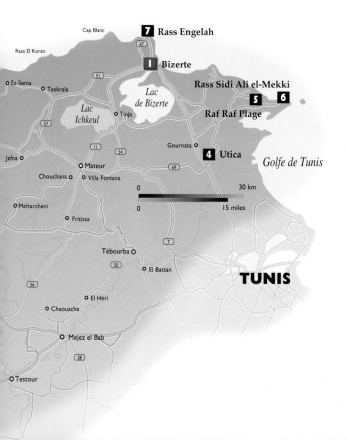

Cap Blanc

7 Rass Engelah

Rass El Koran

67

1 Bizerte

51

Es-Sema ○   ○ Teskrala

*Lac
de Bizerte*

Rass Sidi Ali el-Mekki

5   **6**

*Lac
Ichkeul*

○ Tinja

Raf Raf Plage

57

Gournata ○   **4** Utica

Jefna ○

54

Golfe de Tunis

○ Mateur

69

Chouchana ○   ○ Villa Fontana

0   30 km

○ Meltarcheni

0   15 miles

○ Fritissa

7

Tébourba ○

50

56

○ El Battan

TUNIS

○ El Héri

○ Chaouache

○ Mejez el Bab

28

○ Testour

The northern area of Tunisia can be explored by car comfortably in three days. Setting off from Tunis you visit Phoenician ruins, white sandy beaches, cork oak forests and the ruins of underground Roman villas before returning to Tunis.

The North in Three Days

Day One

Morning

Travel north out of Tunis on Autoroute (Motorway) 8 for 33km, then turn right at Route 69. Continue for 2km until you reach **4 Utica** (➤ 78). This old Carthaginian city was also important in Roman times. Visit the site and inspect the baths and villa ruins with their mosaics.

Follow Route 69 northwards. This leads to the coast and the long, white stretch of sand at **5 Raf Raf Plage** (right, ➤ 78). Enjoy a seafood lunch at any of the beachfront restaurants.

Afternoon

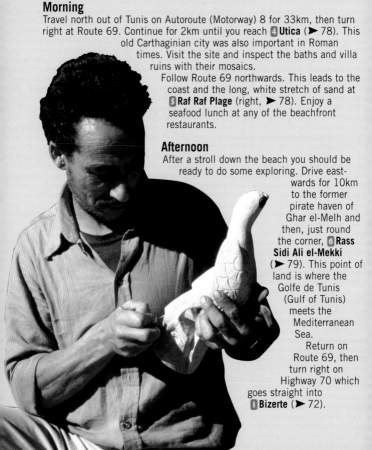

After a stroll down the beach you should be ready to do some exploring. Drive eastwards for 10km to the former pirate haven of Ghar el-Melh and then, just round the corner, **6 Rass Sidi Ali el-Mekki** (➤ 79). This point of land is where the Golfe de Tunis (Gulf of Tunis) meets the Mediterranean Sea.

Return on Route 69, then turn right on Highway 70 which goes straight into **7 Bizerte** (➤ 72).

Evening
Drive a couple of kilometres out of town on the Route de la Corniche to a restaurant called Le Petit Mousse (➤ 83) where you can dine on the terrace and enjoy the view and the cool sea breeze.

Day Two

Morning
In Bizerte, explore the old *kasbah* (fortress) and the quaint quays of the old town.

Drive south out of town by the pleasant hilly country road that leads to Lac Ichkeul (Lake Ichkeul), a picturesque spot for a picnic with its lake and waterfall.

Afternoon
Follow Highway 7 via Sejenane to **2 Tabarka** (➤ 74). At the marina you can organise a 2-hour boat trip to the coral maze known as Tunnels Reef. An afternoon of snorkelling should give you an appetite.

Evening
Enjoy dinner at Porto Corallo harbour in one of the fine seafood establishments such as Touta (➤ 84).

Day Three

Morning
Take a stroll along the esplanade to view the strange rock formations called Les Aiguilles (The Needles) and the old harbour. Leave Tabarka via **8 Aïn Draham** (left, ➤ 79) on Autoroute 17.

Afternoon
Drive through lovely wooded scenery towards **3 Bulla Regia** (➤ 76). Spend the afternoon exploring the Roman ruins of this fascinating site.

Evening
Head south to Jendouba then turn eastwards on Autoroute 6 which leaves you about a 2-hour drive back to Tunis. However, you might decide to spend the night in **10 Béja** (➤ 80) 40km northeast of Jendouba, in which case Hotel Vaga is a good option.

❶ Bizerte

Standing proudly as Africa's northernmost port, Bizerte has always been destined strategically to play a historical role. Over the years, it has been home to Phoenicians and Romans, pirates and fishermen. The largest town on Tunisia's northern coast, Bizerte, in Arabic *Banzart*, retains its elegant old-world charm and nowadays many more visitors are discovering the town on their way to some of the country's prime beaches.

Originally an ancient Phoenician settlement, called Hippo Diarrhytus, Bizerte's inner harbour on the lake, Lac de Bizerte, made it particularly valuable. After the Arab conquest in AD 661 it came to be known as Banzart. The town was occupied between 1535 and 1572 by the Spanish Habsburgs but then seized by the Ottoman Empire and – with its useful hiding place for ships – became a haunt of Barbary corsairs (► 12).

Under French control in the 1890s a 1.5km-long canal was built replacing the old channel, creating a harbour and arsenal at Sidi Abdallah. It was the base at Bizerte that caused troubles in 1961 between the French and President Bourguiba, since France wanted to retain it. The president asked for its return, which was ignored, and fighting broke out. France eventually relinquished Bizerte in 1963, but only after an ugly struggle in which many were killed.

The chief resources around Bizerte include cork oak forests, wheat, livestock and vineyards. It is now partly an old fishing harbour, still active with colourful boats and fishermen repairing their nets. The town is surrounded by neatly paved quays, and the streets are lined with elaborate street lamps, low white buildings, shops and cafés. The harbour entrance is guarded by an immense, solid-looking 17th-century fortress or **kasbah**. Another fort opposite, called Sidi el-Hanni, houses the **Musée Oceanographique** (Oceanographic Museum). Inside the *médina* a gateway with a twisting defensive entrance leads in to the 17th-century **Jemaa al-Kasbah** (The Great Mosque), which survives today with its octagonal minaret (closed to non-Muslims). Above the *médina* on boulevard Hassan en-Nouri is another Turkish fortress called **Fort d'Espagne**, with good views over the town. The area around the canal and the marina is an attractive spot for a stroll and there are several hotels and restaurants on the route de la Corniche, which runs along the beach all the way through to Cap Bizerte.

Brightly painted houses surround the old corsair harbour

TAKING A BREAK

At the southern end of the beach you'll see the Club Nautique. Inside, there's **Le Sport Nautique** (► 83), a restaurant which serves international cuisine. It's an excellent spot to eat, drink and enjoy the view across the harbour and the beach.

🚩 181 D4
✉ 66km northwest of Tunis
🚌 To Tunis every half-hour from quai Tarik Ibn Zaid
🚉 Station on rue de Rinja
ℹ 1, rue de Constantinople
☎ 72 432897

Kasbah
✉ Just beyond the old harbour

Musée Oceanographique
✉ avenue Habib Bourguiba
🕐 Tue–Sun 9–12, 2:30–8 (2:30–6 in winter)
💰 Inexpensive

Fort d'Espagne
✉ boulevard Hassan en Nouri
🕐 Daily
💰 Free

BIZERTE: INSIDE INFO

Top tip If you are here in July or August you can catch the **spectacular cultural festival** which takes place each evening at the Fort d'Espagne. The festival includes musical and theatrical performances.

One to miss The **Musée Oceanographique** doesn't really offer anything more than small and familiar aquatic life.

② Tabarka

This region to the west near the Algerian border is sometimes called the Coral Coast. The clear limpid waters are perfect for diving, snorkelling, sailing and windsurfing. Only 20 minutes away by boat lies an undersea world known as Tunnels Reef, where a fascinating maze of corals awaits you.

Tabarka is developing into an important resort town, with a popular *zone touristique*. Starting some 20 years ago Tunisia began investing heavily here with an international airport 14km outside the town, a marina, a casino, new hotels and an 18-hole golf course. With its lovely blue bay dominated by the tree-covered hills of the Kroumirie range, and lined with white buildings and a broad sandy beach, Tabarka is certainly a pleasant spot. The old port has been developed into a marina called Porto Corallo. There is a diving club, **Club du Plongée du Yachting Club**, at the marina where you can organise scuba-diving, day trips and tours to the reefs. Alternatively you can get information about tours or other transportation from the **Tourist Information Office**.

Apart from the ever popular Tunnels Reef, L'archipel de la Galite (Archipelago of La Galite) is a particularly beautiful

A windswept tree clings to the cliffs near the ancient trading post of Tabarka

spot for a day trip including diving, snorkelling or fishing. This small archipelago of seven islands is 60km from the port so you'll need a speedboat and plenty of sun block. The islands are home to what remains of some old Roman tombs and you might also see rare monk seals lounging on the rocks.

Facing each other across the entrance of the old harbour is a tortured-looking group of rocks called Les Aiguilles (The Needles) and an imposing fortress built by the Genoese when Barbarossa (▶ 14) the pirate surrendered Tabarka to them in 1540.

The town's main road, avenue Bourguiba, contains some of the top hotels, also several beachside restaurants. As well as watersports activities, Tabarka is popular for trekking and horse-riding. Ask at the hotels for information.

Tabarka is also a centre for wild boar hunting in the winter in the surrounding cork forests. Just outside town there is a small museum called the **Musée du Liège** (Museum of Cork) which tells you everything you need to know about this natural resource and sells a fine range of cork souvenirs.

TAKING A BREAK

The marina area at Porto Corallo makes an ideal spot for lunch or dinner. Although there are several good choices of restaurants, **Le Pirate** (▶ 84) is probably the best. Enjoy the sunset over the harbour and the fort with a glass of white wine and a delicious seafood meal.

🔢 180 B4
✉ 170km west of Tunis
🚌 Up to nine buses daily to Tunis
✈ Tabarka Airport, 14km east of the town
🛈 32 avenue Bourguiba ☎ 78 670111

Club du Plongée du Yachting
✉ Porto Corallo ☎ 78 644478

Musée du Liège
✉ 2km down Highway 17 towards Aïn Draham
🕐 Tue–Sun 7–1, 3–6 (8–12, 2–5 in winter)
🎟 Free

TABARKA: INSIDE INFO

Top tip A visit to Tabarka in July will coincide with **three festivals**: Fête du Corail (Coral Festival); Université de l'Été, which is a music and comedy festival; and an international jazz festival.

3 Bulla Regia

In the hills just above the wheat lands of the central Mejerda river valley, are the ruins of the old Numidian town of Bulla Regia. Occupied from the neolithic period, it became the capital of one of the three small Numidian kingdoms after the death of King Massinissa (➤ 8). The town was annexed to the Roman Empire by Emperor Hadrian in the 2nd century AD. Bulla Regia was eventually abandoned after the Arab invasion in the 7th century

At its zenith Bulla Regia was the centre of grain production. The Mejerda River provided the water needed for wheat cultivation in these hot dry lands. Olives were also an important product, making the town, in Roman times, one of the richest in the province. The merchants and nobles therefore could afford opulent homes and their refined mosaics are some of Tunisia's best.

The Underground Villas

The most extraordinary feature of Bulla Regia's way of life was the construction of substantial underground villas on the terraces of the hill called Jebel Rebia by the Romans. One storey above ground and one storey below, the houses were built as such so that citizens could remain cool in this very hot region.

Fortunately, this subterranean construction style helped to preserve much of the history, so nowadays you can see a good deal of the layout and even complete rooms underground. The local gentry adorned these dwellings with lovely mosaics, and several have been left intact in their original positions.

The oldest villa excavated is called the **Maison de la Pêche** (House of Fishing), from a mosaic depicting fishermen. Another, with

Terracotta columns in the interior of the House of the Hunt

small well-preserved vaulted underground chambers, is the **Maison du Tresor** (House of the Treasure). The **Maison de la Chasse** (House of the Hunt), is also still intact with mosaic floors and a colon-naded underground court opening on to several rooms, while the **Maison d'Amphitrite** (House of Amphitrite), Greek goddess of the sea, is named for its mosaics featuring the gods of the sea.

The Memmian Baths

The Memmian Baths, close to the main entrance to Bulla Regia, were built between AD 220 and 240. They were named after an ancient inscription was discovered in dedication to one Julia Memmia, the apparent patron of the baths *"…by which she both beautified her home town and looked after the health of the citizens…"*

Close to the main public areas, the marketplace and the forum are the ruins of the temples dedicated to Isis and Apollo. There is also a Christian basilica with mosaic floors and apses still visible.

A section of the surviving seating in the theatre built between AD 160 and 180

TAKING A BREAK

The nearest good cafés and restaurants are found in Jendouba, 9km to the south of Bulla Regia.

🚩 180 B3
✉ 9km north of Jendouba, 60km south of Tabarka
☎ 78 630554
🕐 Daily 8–7 (winter: Tue–Sun 8:30–5:30)
🚌 To Jendouba from Tunis or Bizerte, then taxi or *louage* 🅿 Inexpensive

---

BULLA REGIA: INSIDE INFO

Top tips The site has only one small café for drinks and **little shade**. You should wear a hat and carry water.
• Arrange to arrive either early in the morning or late in the afternoon to **avoid the midday sun**.

In more depth A collection of fine statues from the temples dedicated to Isis and Apollo and also some of the best mosaics from the site are now preserved in the **Musée du Bardo** (➤ 60).

At Your Leisure

4 Utica

The former port of Utica is the oldest Phoenician settlement on the coast, founded perhaps in the 8th century BC. It was second only to Carthage among the Phoenician cities of Tunisia, and during the Third Punic War (149–146 BC) was occupied by the Roman general, Scipio Africanus Minor, who used it as a bridgehead for his attack on Carthage.
From the mud of the Oued Mejerda (River Mejerda) sections of the Roman city have been recovered, 3km from the modern town. Most monumental are the public baths. There are also paved roads and the remains of several houses which must have belonged to rich Roman citizens. Among these is the important villa now called the Maison de la Cascade (House of the Waterfall), named for the fountain in its courtyard pond.

About 800m before the ruins a small museum exhibits objects found during the excavations, including Punic material from the 8th century BC onwards that proves the settlement's ancient roots. There are stone funerary caskets, ostrich shell amulets with eyes drawn on them,

Site of the Great Baths at Utica

and Greek and Italian pottery. The Roman room contains statues, terracotta, mosaic fragments and inscriptions. A pond in the garden is floored with a seascape mosaic, depicting Neptune with lobster claws protruding from his head.

🚹 181 D4 ✉ 30km southeast of Bizerte 🕐 Tue–Sun 8–6 (8–5 in winter) 🚌 Regular bus services between Tunis and Bizerte 💰 Inexpensive

5 Raf Raf Plage

East of Bizerte, in a secluded cove, Raf Raf Plage (Raf Raf Beach) is a fine unspoilt sandy crescent overlooked by the hill of Jebel Nadour and a small village with white houses. Out to sea, resembling an emerging submarine, is the small island of Pilau, a rocky outcrop ideal for snorkelling and fishing. Along the beach front, pinewood trees provide attractive shade and there are several restaurants. There is little else to do at Raf Raf Plage except enjoy the sun, sea and sand.

Near here at Ghar el-Melh (Salt Cave), Holy Roman Emperor Charles V landed before his capture of Tunis

n 1535. This was a haven for pirates
hen and the town was attacked by
English admiral Robert Blake, among
others, in 1654 (➤ 13).

🔶 181 D4 ✉ 38km east of Bizerte

6 Rass Sidi Ali el-Mekki

The beach of Sidi Ali el-Mekki lies
on a headland poking into the sea
and separates the Mediterranean
from the Gulf of Tunis. This charming spot, which attracts relatively few
visitors, offers peace and quiet, the
occasional café and some small
straw-built lodgings.

A Muslim holy man called Sidi el-
Mekki is buried in a tomb inside the
mountain near by, which is honey-
combed with passages. Non-Muslims
cannot enter, but a terrace above
offers splendid views.

🔶 181 D4 ✉ 44km east of Bizerte

7 Rass Engelah

Rass (an Arabic word meaning
"head") Engelah is the northernmost
point on the African continent. West
of Bizerte and just beyond Cap Blanc
on the north coast, the head has an
attractive Moorish-style lighthouse.
The nearby village of Bechateur, several kilometres inland, is a substantial Roman site, unexcavated as yet,
but with ruins in evidence on
the hill.

🔶 181 D4 ✉ 6km north of Bizerte

8 Aïn Draham

Aïn Draham nestles in the hills by
the Algerian border, in a beautiful
region of cork oak and pine forests.
It shares with Tabarka the potential

A small fishing boat at Raf Raf Plage

for hiking and wild boar hunting in
season. From Tabarka, driving south
through the Oued el-Kebir valley,
you pass through lovely scenery to
reach the small mountain town. It's a
quaint resort with chalets which benefit from the cool pleasant climate.
You can walk in the hills, and both
Jebel Bir (Hill of the Well) and the
Col des Ruines are summits offering
lovely views of the surrounding
forests.

🔶 180 B3 ✉ 20km south of Tabarka

9 Chemtou and Thuburnica

The ruins of Chemtou and
Thuburnica are to the west of Bulla
Regia. Chemtou (originally called
Simitthus) is a first-century AD foundation of Roman Emperor Augustus.
The area was renowned for a particular dark yellowish marble, stained
with iron oxide, which was highly
valued.

Thuburnica, on an unsurfaced
road west of Chemtou, is remote, but
worth the effort for those who like
Roman ruins and scenery. The town
was originally founded by General
Marius in the 1st century BC. There is
a splendid bridge, still intact and
10m high, which stretches across a
river. Other ruins include temples to
Juno, Concord and the Four Seasons,
as well as the vestiges of a two-storey
mausoleum.

Chemtou

🔶 180 B3 ✉ 10km west of Bulla Regia
on Road 59 ⏰ Open access 🎫 Free

Thuburnica

🔶 180 B3 ✉ 14km west of Chemtou,
15km from the Algerian border ⏰ Open
access 🎫 Free

❿ Béja

Béja, situated in the hills north of the Oued Mejerda valley, was designated by an Arab geographer as the granary of Tunis in the 11th century. Inland from the wet coastal plain the area's agricultural potential doubtless explains why Béja was built here. The town, which the Phoenicians originally named Vacca, was sacked during the Vandal invasions in the 5th century but was reconstructed after Byzantium reconquered the region. The walls of the 7th-century fortress still stand on the steep hillside, and the old *médina* survives. Béja prospered under the Turks who used it as a local administrative and military centre. In colonial times the French built a church here, its white walls and red roofs topped by an attractive tower.

Modern Béja maintains a flour mill, sugar refineries and an

Magnificent forests clothe the hills around the mountain village of Aïn Draham

agricultural research station. Its main street is the rue Kheireddine, and a square, the place Abdel Kader, contains a number of well-shaded cafés. You'll also find the *médina*, which is rich in spices and food, and a number of other interesting shopping streets. There is a spring and the shrine of a *marabout* (holy man) at Bab al-Ain (Gate of the Spring) on Béja's main road.

🚻 180 C3 ✉ 110km west of Tunis
🚌 Regular service from Tunis
🚆 Seven trains daily to and from Tunis

Local shoppers on Béja's main street

Where to... Stay

Prices
Expect to pay for a standard double room per night
£ under TD50   **££** TD50–TD100   **£££** over TD100

Outside of Bizerte and Tabarka the choice of accommodation in the north is limited. For a trip to Bulla Regia it's best to make sure you've left yourself enough time to get back to either Aïn Draham or Tabarka. If you do find yourself stuck for time there are a couple of basic hotels in Jendouba, 9km to the south.

AÏN DRAHAM

Hotel Nour el-Aïn ££

A hotel favoured by hunters, so expect it to be very busy during the hunting season. It's beautifully situated near the woods with excellent views over the town. There are 60 rooms, a restaurant, a covered, heated swimming pool, necessary if you want to swim here in the winter season, a *hammam* (Turkish bath) and a fitness centre.

➕ 180 B3 ⊠ Col des Ruines, 2km north of Aïn Draham, ☎ 78 655600; fax: 78 655185

BIZERTE

Bizerta Resort £££

On the Corniche at Bizerte there is a selection of hotels constituting a small *zone touristique*. The most prominent, and the best, is the Bizerta Resort, a large, comfortable 100-room beach hotel. Many rooms and suites have sea views. It has a pleasant garden café, and indoor and outdoor swimming pools.

➕ 181 D4 ⊠ route de la Corniche ☎ 72 436966; fax: 72 422955; email: hbizerta@gnet.tn

Corniche £

A very comfortable hotel on what is the best part of the beach. It usually caters for groups and therefore there's quite a variety of evening entertainment, with local cultural shows. Facilities include a large pool, a restaurant and for those wanting to keep fit there's daily aerobics classes.

➕ 181 D4 ⊠ 244 route de la Corniche, 4km north of town ☎ 72 431831; 72 422515; email: cornichepalace@hotmail.com

Continental £

If you are looking for a clean, no-frills hotel in the centre of town, the Continental is ideal. Unfortunately there are no hot showers, although this should not pose a problem for most of the year. The rooms can be a little noisy with the hotel located on one of Bizerte's busier streets. Facilities are limited, but the Continental is well placed for exploring the old traditional quarter of the town around the port.

➕ 181 D4 ⊠ rue d'Istanbul ☎ 72 431436

Le Petit Mousse ££

This very small and intimate 12-room hotel, across the road from the beach, is a big contrast to the larger Bizerte hotels. The management is both friendly and efficient, and therefore it is a popular place, so it's best to book well in advance. Though it can be rather noisy from the traffic along the beach road, it has the extra attraction of a very good restaurant serving French and international cuisine.

➕ 181 D4 ⊠ route de la Corniche, 6km north of town ☎ 72 432185; fax: 72 437595

Sidi Salem ££

A great location for both beach and town, just 200m east of Bizerte's *kasbah*. Unfortunately, in the summer the hotel's room rates rocket, often costing more than twice as much as at any other time of the year. Amenities include an attractive pool and tennis courts.

🟥 181 D4 ⊠ Sidi Salem Complex, Sidi Salem Beach ☎ 72 420365; fax: 72 420380

RAF RAF PLAGE

Dalia £

This small, comfortable hotel is really the only choice at Raf Raf. It's well placed near the beach, with its own restaurant; the Turkish coffee is excellent. Room rates in winter drop dramatically as you are likely to have the hotel to yourself. The Dalia is a good choice for people looking for a quieter, less crowded destination.

🟥 181 D4 ⊠ On the seafront road ☎ 72 441688

---

of fine restaurants near the quays of the inner harbour basin. The upper rooms, though tiring to get to with no lift, are pleasant if plain, and offer small balconies with views over the old harbour and the Genoese fort.

🟥 180 B4 ⊠ 11 avenue 7 Novembre 1987 ☎ 78 670039

Les Mimosas ££

Set on a hill slightly to the southeast of the town with a view over the bay and harbour, Les Mimosas is a friendly, low-key hotel. It has around 80 rooms, a circular pine-shaded swimming pool, tennis court and a pleasant restaurant.

🟥 180 B4 ⊠ Near the turn off to Aïn Draham on the Bizerte road ☎ 78 673018; fax: 78 673276

Méhari Tabarka £££

The Méhari is another huge hotel complex in Tabarka's *zone touristique*. It has similar amenities to the Abou Nawas Montazah, with the addition of a balneotherapy centre

---

TABARKA

Abou Nawas Montazah £££

In the *zone touristique* outside the town, beyond the Porto Corallo marina, the large Abou Nawas Montazah offers superb facilities. An Olympic-sized swimming pool tops the list, but there are also five tennis courts, a diving centre, gymnasium, archery, rifle shooting and a very good beachfront. Children's activities are many and varied, including a giant chessboard. It's also close to the Tabarka Golf Club (▶ 86).

🟥 180 B4 ⊠ Route Touristique, 4km east of Tabarka ☎ 78 673532; fax: 673530; email: montazah@abounawas.com.tn

Hôtel de la Plage £

For a modern, comfortable hotel in town, the Hôtel de la Plage, situated opposite the new residential apartment block next to the harbour, is very convenient. It is close to a selection of shops, and to a number

---

(Jacuzzi, hydro-massage tubs and a Turkish bath) plus an indoor as well as outdoor swimming pool. All rooms have satellite television and air-conditioning.

🟥 180 B4 ⊠ Route Touristique, 3km east of Tabarka ☎ 78 670184; fax: 78 673943; www.goldenyasmin.com

Royal Golf £££

One of Tabarka's best all-inclusive resorts set in an attractive forest. The beach is approximately 300m away. All rooms and suites are equipped with satellite television, air-conditioning and balconies. Facilities include access to a superb golf course with 11 of the holes winding through the forest; the other seven hug the coastline. The wide choice of watersports – deep-sea diving, sailing, windsurfing – and other sporting activities makes the Royal Golf probably the best value choice in the *zone touristique*.

🟥 180 B4 ⊠ Zone Touristique, ☎ 78 673899; fax: 78 673838; www.royal-golf-tunisia.com

Where to...
Eat and Drink

Prices

Expect to pay per person for a standard three-course meal, excluding drinks and service charges

£ under 15DT   ££ 15–30DT   £££ over 30DT

The tourist restaurants in the Tabarka area are accustomed to catering for their visitors' varied tastes, but most other areas of the North are not well represented with this type. Bizerte has many restaurants along its extended Corniche and many of them are good, but the town's Le Sport Nautique is probably the best restaurant in Northern Tunisia. Restaurants outside the *zone touristique* rarely sell alcoholic drinks.

AÏN DRAHAM

Beauséjour Hotel ££

Once known for its *marcassin* (wild boar piglet), the Beauséjour these days serves its clientele a more mundane, less exotic *carte du jour*. Try the excellent *mloukhia*, a lamb or beef dish made with the leaf of the *mloukhia* plant. Wild boar might still find its way on to the table during the hunting season, but you will probably have to ask for it. The restaurant also has two bars, one of them usually the pre-

serve of the locals, but visitors are welcome.

✚ 180 B3 ⬛ avenue Habib Bourguiba (centre of town) ☎ 78 655363 ⊚ Daily 11–2:30, 5–11

BIZERTE

L'Eden ££

The Eden is popular with locals and on a Saturday night there is usually some quite boisterous musical entertainment going on. If you prefer a quiet dinner then this is not really the place to come. During the summer months meals are served outside on the lovely flower covered terrace, the rest of the year inside in the dining room. Highly recommended is the seafood and fresh fish, especially the scampi.

✚ 181 D4 ⬛ 4km along route de la Corniche, opposite the Corniche Hotel ☎ 78 439023 ⊚ Daily 11–2:30, 6–11

Le Petit Mousse ££

Most of the reasonable restaurants in Bizerte are out of town on the route de la Corniche, and Le Petit Mousse has the reputation of being perhaps the best of them. The beach is just over the road, and there is a terrace or garden for dining outside. The upstairs dining room serves a wide variety of French dishes and during the summer months the terrace is turned into a barbecue area serving grilled fish, various meats and kebabs, and pizzas. There is a reasonable wine menu.

✚ 181 D4 ⬛ route de la Corniche, 6km north of town ☎ 72 432185 ⊚ Daily 11–2:30, 5:30–11

Le Sport Nautique £££

This restaurant is the best choice in Bizerte; in fact it comes highly recommended by a number of French food and drink magazines. It's very well situated, beside the Club Nautique overlooking the attractive harbour. Lunchtime is an especially good time to visit as there is a lot going on around the canal and harbour. The Nautique is famous for its exceptional fish *couscous* and a number of superb seafood dishes including lobster and steamed fillet of sole. All seafood served is straight out of the sea, and the management is both conscious and proud of their restaurant's reputation which they strive to preserve.

🚹 181 D4 ⊠ boulevard Habib Bougatfa, Port de Plaisance ☎ 72 433262 ☻ Daily 11–3, 6–11

Restaurant du Bonheur ££

The Bonheur is renowned for its excellent fish dishes. The *rouget* (red mullet) served with a fresh Mediterranean salad and plate of french fries can be very satisfying. They also pride themselves on their various *couscous* preparations. A recently opened section of the restaurant offers air-conditioning and can be a relief in the summer. The Bonheur serves wine and other alcoholic drinks.

🚹 181 D4 ⊠ 31 rue Thaalbi ☎ 72 431047 ☻ Mon–Sat 11–3, 6–11, Sun lunch only; closed Ramadan

Andalous £

Many of the mid-range hotels offer good-value set meals in their restaurants. The Andalous is no exception with a hearty three-course set menu. Other dishes to look for include *loup de mer* (sea perch), lamb cutlets and *mirmiz* (stewed mutton). Alcoholic beverages and an assortment of wines are also served with meals.

🚹 180 B4 ⊠ Andalous Hotel, avenue Habib Bourguiba ☎ 78 670600 ☻ Daily 11–3, 6–10.30

Les Aiguilles £

Les Aiguilles, once a bank, can be found in the hotel of the same name, a fine old colonial building. It serves a number of Tunisian specialities such as *shakshuka* (vegetable soup), and plenty of fresh seafood. There is a choice of dining areas; opt for either the terrace or the attractively decorated inside dining room.

🚹 180 B4 ⊠ 18 avenue Habib Bourguiba ☎ 78 673789 ☻ Daily 10.30–2, 5–10

Les Mimosas £

Les Mimosas is another hotel restaurant up on the hill overlooking the bay. If you decide to eat here at lunchtime you will be entitled to use the swimming pool. The food is unexceptional, but the view over the town and port more than compensates for this. The menu is basic local dishes with some international additions such as *spaghetti aux fruits de mer* (seafood spaghetti).

🚹 180 B4 ⊠ Near the turn off to Ain Draham on the Bizerte road ☎ 78 673018; fax: 78 673276 ☻ Daily 11–2.30, 6–11

Le Pirate ££

In the Porto Corallo area, out by the harbour, Le Pirate features a number of good fish dishes and its *chakchouka* (similar to a stuffed omelette) can be very good.

Tabarka is a busy port which means that seafood features high on the restaurant's specialities' list, and there is also quite a good choice of wines.

🚹 180 B4 ⊠ Porto Corallo Complex ☎ 78 670061 ☻ Daily 11–2.30, 5.30–11.30

Touta ££

Touta is another first-rate harbour restaurant with an upstairs dining room and terrace. The terrace has a good view over the harbour and across to the Genoese fort. Fish provides the main emphasis of the menu, although some dishes like the *crevettes royales* (king prawns) can be quite expensive for the average visitor. Fresh oysters are occasionally served depending on whether the right boat docked in the harbour that morning. If you don't feel like seafood, the beefsteak and French fries are dependable.

🚹 180 B4 ⊠ Porto Corallo Complex ☎ 78 671018 ☻ Daily 11–2.30, 6–11.30; closed Ramadan

Where to... Shop

SOUQS

As usual in Tunisia, the first place to go shopping is the local **souq**. Here you will find a wide range of local handicrafts for sale in picturesque surroundings reminiscent of past centuries, as well as the haunting aromas of spice and perfume markets.

If you are in a hurry, or if bargaining doesn't appeal, then you should turn to the local branch of the government-run, fixed price Offices Nationales de l'Artisanat Tunisien (ONAT) or Société de Commercialisation des Produits de l'Artisanats (SOCOPA). More frequently than any other location in the north these can be found in Bizerte.

Bizerte is the largest town on the north coast and as such has the best shopping facilities. The Bizerte branch of **ONAT** is at quai Khemais Ternane (tel: 72 431091), close by the old port off place Bouchoucha (next to the Tunisian Tourist Office). For modern goods ranging from designer clothes to photographic equipment head for the **Ville Nouvelle**, especially around rue ibn Khaldoun and rue 1 Juin 1955. The **Central Market** on rue 2 Mars 1934 and avenue Taïeb Mehiri is well stocked with goods of every description, from spices and vegetables to T-shirts and jeans. Near by on the north side of rue 2 Mars 1934 the **Monoprix Supermarket** is the best place in town for imported foods, wines, salami and other delicacies. There are tourist shops selling typically Tunisian souvenirs in the *medina* (which is the heart of the old town) and near the huge *kasbah*. Finally – at least for atmosphere even if you're not going to make a

purchase – the **Fish Market** and **Harbour Market** are both located by the Mosque of Sidi Abdullah on place Bouchoucha.

Tabarka is less of a shopping centre than Bizerte, but still the second most important commercial centre on the north coast. The **Central Market** is near the junction of avenue Habib Bourguiba and rue Farhad Hached. Close by, at the junction of avenue Habib Bourguiba and avenue d'Algérie, is a large supermarket selling imported wines and luxury foodstuffs. Further north, on avenue 7 Novembre 1987, is Tabarka's **Monoprix Supermarket**, a good place to stock up on imported foodstuffs. Some shops in Tabarka, the "capital of the Coral Coast", sell coral jewellery, but the local red coral is a protected species because of the ravages collecting has inflicted on the coral beds. There are locally carved wooden objects, animals and birds, and briar pipes, that you can take home as souvenirs.

Outside Tabarka, 2km from the town towards Aïn Draham, is the **Cork Museum**, in the cork forest area, where the processes of cork making from the thick spongy bark of the cork oak is explained. Here you can buy souvenirs made from cork.

Aïn Draham is famous for its carpets and *kilim* woven rugs. These are for sale at **Les Tapis de Kroumirie**, above the Ministère des Affaires Sociales. Prices are fixed, but not overly expensive. It's a great place to visit, and if your interest in the craft of carpet weaving goes beyond purchasing or collecting, there are about ten looms in operation where you can watch them being woven, or even photograph your own rug as it is being produced.

In **Béja** the **Souq el-Nehasach** sells various local handicrafts including, particularly hand-woven woollen blankets called *kilim* for which this area of the country is renowned.

Where to...
Be Entertained

NIGHTLIFE

Nightclubs are not a great feature in the North. For diversions of this kind – dancing involving both sexes, drinking alcohol, floor shows and even belly dancing – it's invariably best to stick to the entertainment provided at all-inclusive resorts. Beyond this, in Bizerte there is a nightclub at the **Corniche Hotel**, 4km out of town on the route de la Corniche (▶ 81). Also in Bizerte, on Saturday evenings, **L'Eden** restaurant on the route de la Corniche (▶ 83) features dining to music by local musicians.

SPORT AND LEISURE

The **Tabarka Golf Club** (tel: 78 671031; fax: 78 671026) has an 18-hole seaside course, open to visitors for a fee of TD50 including green fees and club hire. **Watersports** are a prominent feature of the northern coast. Windsurfing, diving and snorkelling are popular at Tabarka, and there are marinas at Tabarka and Bizerte. The **Club du Plongée du Yachting Club** at Tabarka port has excellent facilities, but you have to join to enjoy them (tel: 78 671478). Scuba diving tuition is available at some of the big beach hotels in the *zone touristique*, notably the **Abou Nawas Montazah** (▶ 82).

Horse-riding is an increasingly popular option in the hills around Tabarka. This is best arranged through the **Hotel Paradise** (tel: 78 673002) out in the *zone touristique*. Equestrian opportunities on offer range from two-hour rides to overnight treks into the forested foothills of the nearby Kroumirie Mountains – though this option is limited to small groups of six and upwards.

Hunting and shooting possibilities exist up in the mountains around Ain Draham and Tabarka between December and February. Hunting permits can be arranged by various hotels in Ain Draham, notably **Hotel les Chênes** (tel: 78 655211; fax: 78 655315) and **Hotel Rihana** (tel: 78 655391; fax: 78 655396), though if hunting is your scene it may be wise to get this arranged in advance through a tour company.

Trekking is an increasingly popular option in the hills around Ain Draham. If you're considering a long trek then be advised that a local guide is essential as maps are scarce and unreliable, while there are hazards such as wild boar in the forests. A popular shorter trek is the forest route by the Col des Ruines, which takes between 2 and 3 hours. Ask at the **Hotel Nour el-Ain** (▶ 81).

The north coast's **Lake Ichkeul National Park** (▶ 162) offers some of the best bird-watching opportunities in North Africa and was designated a UNESCO World Heritage Site in 1977. For the serious naturalist it is a destination not to be missed.

FESTIVALS

Tabarka hosts a renowned **jazz festival** in July. Details can be obtained from the town's tourism office on boulevard 7 Novembre (tel: 78 671491).

The town of Testour, 75km southwest of Tunis, was built in the early 17th century by Andalucian exiles who set up a silk and ceramic industry that still survives today. It stages an annual *maalouf festival* in July, *maalouf* music being part of the old Andalucian heritage in Tunisia.

Cap Bon and the Sahel

Getting Your Bearings

Cap Bon is the northernmost point of a hilly limestone peninsula which points like a finger out into the Mediterranean Sea towards Sicily. The main centres include Nabeul, a famous pottery and handicraft centre; the fishing port of Kelibia; and Hammamet, a small port that has developed into a major beach resort.

The Sahel stretches along the eastern coast down as far as the Golfe de Gabès. This is the land of olive groves and old port towns such as Sousse and Sfax.

The hilly peninsula is very fertile, and its Mediterranean climate offers rainfall sufficient for hearty crops of citrus fruits, olives and vineyards. Pepper, essential for the hot *harissa* sauce, also grows here. An unusual site on the peninsula is Kerkouane, remarkable for the discovery of an abandoned Phoenician town of some size and importance.

The main seaside towns are Sousse, Monastir, Sfax and Mahdia, which was once the capital of the whole Tunisian region. Offshore from Sfax you can take a boat out to the beautiful Îles Kerkennah, or if you head a little inland you will come across the incredible Roman amphitheatre of El Jem, one of the chief ancient sites in all of Tunisia for sheer spectacle.

★ Don't Miss

At Your Leisure

Previous page: The 6th-century Byzantine fort overlooking the harbour and village of Kelibia

Left: Stuffed camels on sale in the shadow of Sousse's 8th-century *ribat*

Île Zembra

Golfe de Tunis

Cap Bon

5 El Haouaria

(27)

6 Kerkouane

Zaoulet El-Mgaiez

Rass el Fartass (26) Tazoghrane

(45) **7** Kelibia

Rass Dourdass

TUNIS

Mraissa

(34) (27) Menzel Temime

Lebna

Menzel Bouzelfa

(1)

Grombalia

Korba

Bou Argoub

Tazerka

(27) **8** Nabeul

Bir Bou

Regba

9 Hammamet

(35)

Pupput

Salloum

Ain Er Rahma

Golfe

de

Hammamet

Enfidaville

(1) Hergla

10 Port el Kantaoui

Kaala Kebira

Kaala Sghira

1 Sousse

(82)

2 Monastir

Golfe de Monastir

El Onk (100) Ouerdanine

Bourjine

Touza

Teboulba

Rass Dimass

Zeramdine

11 Mahdia

(87) (96)

Ksour

Essaf

Salatka

Rass Salatka

Tielsa (87)

Souassi

3 El Jem

Chorbane

Rass Kaboudia

Rass Jezira

El Hencha

(119)

Ouled Bou Smir

(82)

Jerbaa

Louza

50 km

Mejen Drej

El Amra

0

(13) (81) (1)

0

25 miles

El Aouabed

El Bedarna

(119)

Mansour

Ech-Chergui

El Ataya

Agareb

Remla

El Abassia

(14)

4 Sfax

Ouled Kacem

S. Ben Sahioun

Ain Fellat

S. Youssef

12 Îles Kerkennah

Mahres

Ech-Chaffar

(1)

Île Kheneiss

Follow the idyllic coastal road and visit some of Tunisia's most popular resorts and beaches. Take in the country's second and third largest cities, Sousse and Sfax, and explore the Roman amphitheatre at El Jem, where gladiators once fought for their lives.

Cap Bon and the Sahel in Three Days

Day One

Morning

Leaving Tunis, drive out southwards and turn northeast on Route 26 along the scenic north side of the Cap Bon peninsula. You will shortly arrive at the market town of Soliman (with its beach area called Soliman Plage). After a brief stop head up the coast to 5 **El Haouaria** (➤ 100) and explore the Grottes Romaines (Roman Caves) by the seaside, then turn south to 6 **Kerkouane** (➤ 100). Here you can visit the unusual excavated Punic settlement, and tour the small but attractive museum.

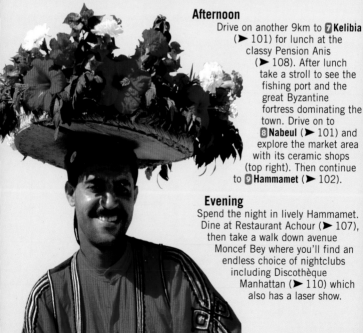

Afternoon

Drive on another 9km to 7 **Kelibia** (➤ 101) for lunch at the classy Pension Anis (➤ 108). After lunch take a stroll to see the fishing port and the great Byzantine fortress dominating the town. Drive on to 8 **Nabeul** (➤ 101) and explore the market area with its ceramic shops (top right). Then continue to 9 **Hammamet** (➤ 102).

Evening

Spend the night in lively Hammamet. Dine at Restaurant Achour (➤ 107), then take a walk down avenue Moncef Bey where you'll find an endless choice of nightclubs including Discothèque Manhattan (➤ 110) which also has a laser show.

Day Two

Morning

Try to visit the Villa Sebastian, also known as the Centre International Culturel, before you embark on the 58km journey to **1 Sousse** (➤ 92). Visit the *médina* and its shops (right), taking time for lunch in one of the local street cafés.

Afternoon

Inspect the Grande Mosquée and the *ribat* or fortified monastery, and be sure you don't miss the Musée de Sousse in the *kasbah*.

Evening

Carry on to **2 Monastir** (below, ➤ 94), 16km away, and spend an evening at the romantic marina. There are several good international restaurants overlooking the quay, but The Captain (➤ 108) is particularly recommended.

Day Three

Morning

Plan to get up early, drive south to **11 Mahdia** (➤ 103) on the coastal Route 82 and have an early seafood lunch at Le Lido (➤ 108) by the port.

Afternoon

Take Route 87 straight to **3 El Jem** (➤ 96). Allow yourself time to explore the wonderful Roman amphitheatre before you drive south about 60km on Autoroute 1 to Sfax.

Evening

After settling into your hotel in **4 Sfax** (➤ 98), spend a relaxing evening at the popular restaurant, Le Baghdad. Alternatively you could try Le Corail (➤ 108) on rue Habib Mazoun, with its excellent seafood.

◻ Sousse

For many visitors Sousse is the quintessential Tunisian city:
it's close to historical sites such as the amphitheatre at El
Jem (► 96), as well as splendid beach resorts such as Port
el Kantaoui (► 103). A coastal town with a mild climate
situated in the olive-growing Sahel region, it was originally
settled by the Phoenicians who named it Hadrametum.

Although Phoenician in origin, Sousse remained busy and
prosperous during Roman, Byzantine and Arab times.
Testimony to this can be found in a most unusual feature –
the **catacombs**, marble tombs from the 2nd to 5th centuries
set in an underground labyrinth of tunnels 5.5km long.

Inside the *médina*

Sousse's *médina*, near the port on sloping terrain, is elegantly
walled and fortified and has twisting, narrow streets. The
original Sea Gate was flattened by the Allies during World
War II. Inside the walls to the north is a 9th-century **ribat**, or
fortified Islamic monastery. Close by is the **Grande Mosquée**
(Great Mosque), originally constructed in 851 by a freed slave

called Mudam. A line of sculptured Kufic Arabic script is
carved on the interior of the walls just below the cornice. It
never had a minaret, probably because the dominating tower
of the *ribat* was near by. The prayer hall, a vast vaulted chamber with two domes, is not open to non-Muslim visitors.

One of the best places in Tunisia for both men and women
to enjoy a Turkish bath is the **Grande Bain Maure Sidi
Bouraoui**. Expect to spend at least two hours here. You will

Fishermen have
used Sousse's
harbour since
Phoenician
times

leave this *hammam* scrubbed, rinsed, massaged and thoroughly refreshed.

Winding down rue Souq el-Reba you come to a very attractive vaulted market, the Souq el-Caïd. At the southwest corner of the *médina* is the 11th- to 16th-century *kasbah* or fort, which is now the **Musée de Sousse**. This is a must for visitors, one of the most attractive museums in all Tunisia and one which rivals the Musée du Bardo in Tunis (➤ 60) for mosaics.

TAKING A BREAK

After that long walk to the top of the *ribat* you'll probably feel you deserve a rest and some refreshment. From the top of the tower you look down on place Farhat Hached, where there is an excellent restaurant called **Le Bonheur**. It serves international cuisine on a terrace that looks directly on to the square.

A sightseer dwarfed by the entrance to the 9th-century *ribat*

➕ 181 E2
✉ 143km south of Tunis
🚂 More than ten services a day from Tunis
ℹ 1 avenue Habib Bourguiba
☎ 73 225157

La Grande Mosquée
➕ 186 C4
✉ rue el-Aghlaba, Médina
🕐 Sat–Thu 8–1
💵 Inexpensive

Musée de Sousse
➕ 186 A1
✉ boulevard Marechal Tito
☎ 73 233695
🕐 Tue–Sun 8–12, 4–7 (9:30–12, 2–6 in winter)
💵 Moderate

Ribat
➕ 186 B4
✉ rue des Martyrs, Médina
🕐 Tue–Sun 8–7 (9–12,

2–6 in winter)
💵 Inexpensive

Grande Bain Maure Sidi Bouraoui
➕ 186 B3
✉ rue el-Aghlaba, Médina
🕐 Daily 6–1 (men only), 1–7 (women only)
💵 Inexpensive

Catacombs
➕ Off map 186 A2
✉ Admission from the rue Aboul Hamed el-Ghazali
🕐 Tue–Sun 8–12, 3–7 (9–12, 2–6 in winter)
💵 Inexpensive

SOUSSE: INSIDE INFO

Top tip If you are in Sousse on a Sunday you'll catch the famous **Sunday market** at Souq el-Ahad. Everything you can think of is for sale, from camels to carpets to computers and more.

2 Monastir

Monastir is the successor of Rous Penna or Ruspinum, a Phoenician and Roman settlement 5km from the present town. What is left of the old walled town of Monastir – the *médina*, the great *ribat* of Harthema and the charming fishing port – make it worth a visit. Apart from its local industries of textiles, salt, soap and olive oil, Monastir lives up to the image of a Tunisian tourist town – revamped, modern and clean.

The *Ribat*

Just before you reach the huge marina, you pass the *ribat* (fortified Islamic monastery), its vast, yellow stone walls towering over the harbour. Built like the Sousse *ribat* by the Aghlabid dynasty, this monastery was founded in 796 by Harthema ibn Ayyun and has since been continually repaired and enhanced. The Monastir *ribat*, with its austere architecture, was used as the set for Franco Zeffirelli's film *Jesus of Nazareth*, as well as the Monty Python comedy *The Life of Brian*. On the upper floor is an old prayer hall which nowadays displays an interesting collection of Islamic Art. If you climb the winding watchtower you will be rewarded with a view over the city, the beach and the 9th-century Great Mosque below.

The gilded dome of Habib Bourguiba's mausoleum

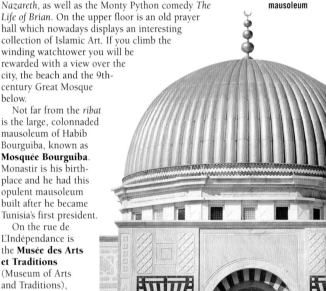

Not far from the *ribat* is the large, colonnaded mausoleum of Habib Bourguiba, known as **Mosquée Bourguiba**. Monastir is his birthplace and he had this opulent mausoleum built after he became Tunisia's first president.

On the rue de L'Indépendance is the **Musée des Arts et Traditions** (Museum of Arts and Traditions), where the lavishly embroidered costumes of newly-weds are exhibited, some dating back 200 years.

Some might regret the loss of part of the *médina* to reconstruction projects, and the sprouting of enormous hotels for seaside holidaying in the *zone touristique*, which stretches 6km north towards Skanès International Airport, but that development was all part of the first flush of enthusiasm for turning Monastir into a major tourist destination. In the case of the popular hotels the tourist boom has, in fact, been a great success. The beaches are usually crowded in high season with European families escaping the winter climes.

TAKING A BREAK

After visiting the *ribat* and taking in an aerial view of Monastir from the tower, go down to route de la Corniche for a delicious ice-cream from one of the vendors at the roadside below the walls.

A group of local men in procession during one of Monastir's many festivals

╬ 181 E2
✉ 160km south of Tunis
🛈 rue de L'Indépendance
☎ 73 461960

Musée des Arts et Traditions
✉ rue de l'Indépendance
🕐 Tue–Sun 9–1, 3–7
💰 Inexpensive

Ribat
✉ Behind route de la Corniche
☎ 73 461272
🕐 Daily 8–7 (9:30–7 in winter)
💰 Moderate

Bourguiba Mosquée
✉ rue de Sidi el Mezzeri
🕐 Not open to visitors

MONASTIR: INSIDE INFO

In more detail In Arabic, *ribat* means a "camp", and the garrisons of these North African *ribats* were composed of **members of religious brotherhoods** called *marabouts* (*marabout* meaning "one who is garrisoned"). *Ribats* were also important for the cultural diffusion of Islam, since the garrisons included lettered warrior monks. Any passing pilgrims from elsewhere in the Islamic world would be received hospitably.

3 El Jem

The chief attraction of El Jem is the imposing Roman amphitheatre, even better preserved than the Colosseum in Rome, and only slightly smaller. The structure, the largest Roman monument in Africa, is a glowing testimony to the wealth and civic pride of the Romans in the Province of Africa during the 3rd century AD.

El Jem, inland between Sousse and Sfax, is an unimpressive modern town built over the ruins of the ancient Roman city of Thysdrus. The surrounding countryside is rather dull and filled only with olive trees, but this explains the extraordinary wealth of the region in ancient times. The town was built between 230 and 238, during the reigns of Alexander Severus and Maximinus, two close successors to the "African emperor" Septimius Severus (➤ 9), and was financed by gold which was acquired from the local cash crop, olives. Thysdrus suffered for its excessive wealth, being sacked in a revolt against Emperor Maximinus in 238.

The soaring tiers of the Roman amphitheatre of Thysdrus

The huge **amphitheatre**, 149m long by 124m wide, was built with blocks brought from quarries 30km away. Water was provided by an underground aqueduct from a source 15km from the town. The amphitheatre's original seating rose tier after tier to 36m, supported on mighty stone arches above the huge oval arena. It is estimated that between 30,000 and 35,000 people could gather here to attend the macabre performances of gladiators battling either wild animals or convicts. Some of the beasts that were regarded in Rome as outlandish exotics were native: the Numidian lion, for example, and African elephants. The vast structure was also used as a fortress at times, and legend claims that it was once held by El Kahina, the female Berber resistance leader who defied the conquering Arabs. Nowadays, in fine contrast, you can attend concerts of symphonic music during the annual festival held in the magnificent setting of the amphitheatre.

You should also take the time to visit the **Musée Archéologique** (Archaeological Museum) just outside El Jem on the road to Sfax. It is worth seeing the mosaics and other ancient artefacts that illustrate Roman life in Africa at this time. Some depict the wild beasts that were once killed in the amphitheatre.

The outer wall of the amphitheatre

TAKING A BREAK

In the main square beside the train station is a pleasant restaurant called **Relais Julius** which serves good food and beer and also offers rooms for the night.

✚ 181 E1
✉ 70km south of Sousse
🚌 Five services a day from Tunis

El Jem Amphitheatre
✉ In the village of El Jem, 70km south of Sousse on Autoroute 1
🕑 Daily 7–7 (8–5 in winter)
🎟 Moderate

Musée Archéologique
✉ 1km south of the amphitheatre on Autoroute 1
🕑 Daily 7–7 (8–5 in winter)
🎟 Included in price of amphitheatre

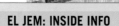

EL JEM: INSIDE INFO

Top tip If you are here in late July or early August you can catch the **El Jem International Music Festival**, when the colosseum is transformed into a spectacular show featuring symphony orchestras and various other musical acts.

4 Sfax

Al-Safaqus or Sfax, another of Tunisia's coastal cities, is surrounded by massive, well-maintained old defensive walls and towers. The town has not become a tourist resort, though the ferry for the Îles Kerkennah leaves from the port here. Between the old town and the port the French laid out a new city with regular streets and some quite striking buildings of Arab-European architectural style. Sfax is an ideal opportunity to witness an authentic Tunisian city where the local people are unaccustomed to tourists and the menus are in Arabic.

Sfax dates from 859, when it was founded close to the Roman site of Taparura. As in the past, olives and fishing form an important part of its economy. Sfax traded afar, and gradually rose to become Tunisia's second city. It desperately resisted the French protectorate imposed in 1881, with the result that it was stormed by French marines causing considerable loss of Tunisian lives.

The walls built by the Aghlabids in the 9th century conceal a real living city of warren-like streets, covered *souqs* and endless activity. Entering by the main gate, Bab Diwan, you

A heavily laden horse-drawn cart on the road to Sfax

can watch furniture-makers, jewellers and tailors at work in their first-floor workshops, or stroll through the covered market streets between the Great Mosque and the rue des Forgerons (Iron Workers Street). There are also a number of fine doorways to old houses and minor mosques, and the minaret of Sidi Amar Kammun in the rue Borj el-Nar. The *kasbah*, in the southwest corner, built over a 9th-century *ribat*, houses a museum of Arab architecture, with some rebuilt fragments of arched galleries and pillars.

The fortified *médina* is a pleasant surprise. The gates pierced into the huge walls, well-equipped with crenellated towers and set off by grass, shrubs and palm trees, welcome you into another world. The main entrance is on avenue Ali Belhouane. The oldest surviving gate is the Bab Jebli, beyond which is a large and lively food market specializing in fish.

In the Ville Nouvelle (New Town) you'll find the **Musée Archéologique** (Archaeological Museum). It is on the ground floor of the splendid colonial Hôtel de Ville (Town Hall), but there is no indication outside that a museum exists there; a pity, since though small it houses some interesting objects, including Roman mosaics from ancient Sfax.

The tortured lines of a large olive wood sculpture in central Sfax

TAKING A BREAK

Close to Bab Diwan, the gate on the southern side of the *médina*, there's a busy little café called **Le Diwan** which is actually built into the ramparts of the *médina* walls. It's a great people-watching spot where you can relax with a coffee or a glass of mint tea.

➕ 181 E1
✉ 270km southeast of Tunis
🚆 Eight services a day from Tunis
⛴ Regular daytime services to Îles Kerkennah

Musée Archéologique
✉ At the junction of avenues Habib Bourguiba and Hedi Chaker
☎ 74 229744
🕐 Tue–Sat 9:30–4:30
💰 Inexpensive

SFAX: INSIDE INFO

Hidden gem The **Dar Jallouli Museum** on rue de la Driba is a médina mansion of the 17th century that once belonged to a prominent family, sometime governors of the city. It gives a good idea of life in the hidden recesses of the old city.

At Your Leisure

5 El Haouaria

Just outside El Haouaria by the coast near the very top of the Cap Bon peninsula are the Grottes Romaines (Roman Caves). Hollowed out over the ages by the different builders of the region, these 24 spectacular caves were sculpted as they were quarried for the yellow-orange limestone so valued by the local Carthaginian, Roman and Byzantine architects. One, Ghar el-Kebir (Big Cave), has a camel sculpted from the rock.

Wildlife is abundant in this area and many birdwatchers come to view the migrant egrets, gulls and waders. Falcons and hawks are greatly admired here – the birds are nurtured from chicks, and exhibited at an annual falconry festival in June, after which they are released.

World Heritage Site. It was originally a Punic town, constructed in the 6th century BC and abandoned in the 3rd century BC. A double ring of walls

Above: The Ghar el-Kebir caves near El Haouaria

Below: The excavations at Kerkouane

➕ 181 E4 ✉ 14km north of Kerkouane
🕐 Daily 8–7 (9–5 in winter)
💶 Inexpensive

6 Kerkouane

In a lovely setting on the eastern coast of the peninsula of Cap Bon is Kerkouane, now listed as a UNESCO

defended it and within were numerous groups of stone-built houses separated by wide streets and squares. The general shape of the town is semicircular, with a sanctuary and temple in the centre. Some of the houses had their own pink cement bathrooms. The harbour area

has long vanished into the sea, where a new sea wall has been built to protect the site.

An interesting museum allows a glimpse of the daily life of this ancient community. It is thought that the population of around 2,500 people was largely engaged in making the fabulously costly Tyrian purple dye from shellfish. The dye was used in colouring various artefacts and the extraction process was lengthy, making it an expensive, highly prized luxury.

🔲 181 E4 ⊠ 14km south of El Haouaria, 9km north of Kelibia on route 27 ☎ 72 294033 🕐 Tue–Sun 9–7 (9–4:30 in winter) 🎫 Inexpensive

7 Kelibia

Kelibia, by the headland called Rass Mostefa, is a fishing town on the lower tip of the Cap Bon peninsula. It remains largely unspoilt, with a good beach about 2km north at Mansourah. By day Kelibia is tranquil, and at night the only noticeable activity is the fishing boats setting out with lamps to attract their catch.

In 256 BC the Romans camped here after defeating the Carthaginian navy. High on a hill, dominating the whole town and its coast, is the massive battlemented wall and bastions of a great Byzantine castle built in the 6th century on older Roman remains. Visitors can walk freely around the fort and enjoy the views from the battlements.

🔲 181 E3 ⊠ 68km north of Hammamet on route 27

8 Nabeul

This Phoenician settlement was destroyed by the Romans in 146 BC, but because of its advantageous position they rebuilt it. It was renamed Neapolis and became the administrative centre of the Cap Bon region.

Apparently there was a factory here for the production of fish sauce, or *garum*, which was a product much loved by the Romans.

Today Nabeul is a centre for pottery and ceramics, together with brick-making, stone-cutting, carving and chalk-quarrying. Oranges, flowers, vines and the manufacture of perfume are also important, as is the influx of tourists to the beaches.

The attractive covered *souq* or market area is overlooked by the domes and white walls of the Grande Mosquée (Great Mosque), with its beautiful high minaret dominating the entire town.

Mint tea: a waiter bears a tray of the ubiquitous beverage

At the Musée Archéologique (Archaeological Museum) you can see mosaics from the Neapolis site that illustrate Homer's *Iliad*, some Punic remains from Kerkouane and numerous other fascinating artefacts of the region.

🔲 181 E3 ⊠ 65km southeast of Tunis

Musée Archéologique
⊠ 44 avenue Habib Bourguiba (opposite the Railway Station)
☎ 72 285509 🕐 Tue–Sun 8–1, 4–7 (9:30–4:30 in winter) 🎫 Inexpensive

🚩 Hammamet

Hammamet's attraction is as a resort for package tours. The town is only an hour from Monastir–Skanès airport. At first, it was a millionaires' paradise, but gradually this changed and Hammamet now figures high on the list of popular beach destinations.

médina is guarded by the *kasbah*, a 13th-century Hafsid fort from which you can survey the city and the coast below. Inside are numerous winding streets, and the Grande Mosquée (Great Mosque). The tomb of a local patron saint, Sidi Bou Hadid, is close to the *kasbah*.

Part of the old *médina* in Hammamet

tions. It has some of the loveliest beaches on the Tunisian Riviera, with many hotels, restaurants, cafés, casinos and discos, and a generally relaxed atmosphere. A *zone touristique* stretches north of the town towards Nabeul. The area's climate is Mediterranean, with delightful summers and relatively mild winters.

Hammamet lies between the old Roman sites of Siagum and Pupput, the latter a prosperous port in the 2nd to 4th centuries. Some of its villas have been excavated, and the baths, fountain courts, underground cisterns and Christian tomb mosaics associated with wealthy Roman life can be seen here.

White domes, arches, shuttered windows and narrow lanes typify Hammamet's old walled seaside *médina*. The main gate is the Bab el-Souq (Market Gate), leading on to the chief thoroughfare, now lined with tourist shops. The *médina* offers an attractive combination of shopping areas and old dwellings characterised by studded doors and an air of secrecy and impenetrability. The

Renowned American architect Frank Lloyd Wright once described the luxurious Hammamet villa of Romanian millionaire George Sebastian as "the most beautiful in the world". Built in the 1920s in a graceful Arabic style, this fabulous house has welcomed guests such as artists Paul Klee and André Gide, as well as Winston Churchill and his adversary, General Erwin Rommel (► 21) who made his headquarters here during World War II. Now open to the public as the Centre International Culturel (International Cultural Centre), the villa has delightful sea views. The entrance ticket also includes coffee served by the arcaded pool. A Festival of the Arts takes place here in July and August.

➕ 181 E3 ✉ 60km southeast of Tunis

Pupput
✉ 6km south of Hammamet on Autoroute 1 🕐 Daily 9–1, 3–7 (9–1, 3–5:30 in winter) 💷 Inexpensive

Centre International Culturel
✉ avenue des Nationes Unies ☎ 72
280065 🕐 Daily 8:30–6 (9–5 in winter)
💷 Inexpensive

🔟 Port el Kantaoui

The flashy Port el Kantaoui ("May all go well") north of Sousse is centred on its new marina. It was developed in the late 1970s as a tourist destination, and it has done well. The port attracts many visitors with its gardens and palm trees, yachts, shops, golf course, camel- and horse-riding, diving and discothèques.

Hotels and restaurants, some overlooking the port, and the boats at anchor in the marina, cater for a prosperous clientele: there are no cheap alternatives in this setting. White villas and clean, modern resorts set amid lush gardens, bougainvillaea, manicured lawns and swimming pools ensure a polished and tailored look. For visitors a safe, secluded feeling is generated within an exotic setting.

➕ 181 E2 ✉ 134km south of Tunis

🔟 Mahdia

Mahdia stands right by the sea on a peninsula pointing east from the Sahel coast, amid olive groves and tomato farms. The town is prospering with tourism, and the hotels and beaches in the *zone touristique* have become very popular, but the fishing-port atmosphere has been retained, and pale blue-painted boats throng the harbour under the gaze of the lighthouse on Cap Afrique. The area leading to the lighthouse contains a very large Muslim cemetery where a few Phoenician tombs still remain. Mahdia has a distinguished history; it was built as the fortress port and capital of the Fatimid dynasty's first caliph, Ubayd Allah al-Mahdi. It is pleasant to stroll through the *médina* and perhaps stop at a vine-shaded café in the small but attractive place du Caire, or pass alongside the graceful façade of the Mosquée Mustapha Hamza to the cafés on the rue des Fatmides. Straight on from the place du Caire and not far from the shore is the simple and elegant gateway of the Grande Mosquée (Great Mosque), built in the 1960s, a replica of the original Fatimid mosque, erected more than 1,000 years ago.

Parasailing at Port el Kantaoui

Throughout the *médina* you will find delightful architectural features, especially elaborate doorways of sculpted stone and carved wood. Up on the heights at the end of the peninsula is the Borj el Kebir, the *kasbah* built by the Turks in the 16th century. There are good views over the town and harbour from here.

🇫 181 E2 ✉ 62km southeast of Sousse 🚌 1 service a day from Tunis, 18 a day from Sousse

Borj el Kebir
✉ rue du Borj 🕐 Tue–Sun 9–12, 2–6 (9:30–4:30 in winter) 💶 Inexpensive

🄑 Îles Kerkennah (Kerkennah Islands)

The place of exile for both ex-General Hannibal and ex-President Bourguiba, the Kerkennah is a group of seven little isles reached by ferry from Sfax. The two main inhabited islands, Chergui and Gharbi, were connected by a causeway in Roman times. There is one road, from Sidi Youssef in the south of Gharbi to El Ataya in the north.

Chiefly surviving by fishing and more recently by tourism, the islands are blessed by cool sea breezes. The local method of fishing uses baskets made of palm fronds which are placed in the shallow waters. The fishermen then strike the surface of the sea with more palm fronds, driving the fish into the baskets.

The most popular attractions are the long, sandy beaches and the fresh seafood, particularly squid. You can rent a bicycle at the main resort, Sidi Frej, and ride out to one of the gorgeous, pristine beaches such as Sisi Fankhal, near Remla. Or take a trip round the islands in a *felucca*, the typical Arab sailing vessel.

🇫 181 F1 ✉ 20km east of Sfax 🚢 Departures every two hours in the summer, 4 services a day in the winter, journey time one hour

Waiting for disembarkation on the ferry to the Kerkennah Islands

Where to... Stay

Prices

Expect to pay for a standard double room per night

£ under TD50   ££ TD50–TD100   £££ over TD100

The Cap Bon region, stretching down to Hammamet and beyond to Sousse, Monastir and Mahdia, is Tunisia's busiest tourist area and therefore packed with accommodation of all standards. Even further south, Sfax and the îles Kerkennah provide some very comfortable, varied places to stay.

EL HAOUARIA

Hôtel l'Épervier ££

The Épervier, which translates into English as 'sparrowhawk' and indicates the local interest in falconry, is simple but agreeable. The hotel reg-ularly plays host to groups of ornithologists. It's situated in the heart of the village just a short distance from the Grottes Romaines (Roman Caves). There is a court-yard inside shaded by orange trees and a large rubber tree. All rooms are air-conditioned and the price includes breakfast.

➕ 181 E4 ✉ 3 avenue Habib Bourguiba ☎ 72 297017; fax: 72 297258

Pension Les Grottes £

Situated near the famous caves and isolated from the town, the Pension Les Grottes exhibits a peculiar castellated architecture. With a 40-bed capacity the pension can become quite busy in the season; it's therefore a good idea to try and book in advance. If you plan to stay more than 15 days the owners offer a free pick-up service from Tunis airport, a very good deal consider-ing the airport is more than 100km away. There are excellent views of the surrounding countryside from the pension's terrace.

➕ 181 E4 ✉ On the road to the caves ☎ 72 297296; email: salem.bouraoui@planet.tn

HAMMAMET

Alya ££

The Alya is a friendly, family-run hotel in a great central location, close to Hammamet's beautifully compact *medina*. Room rates vary enormously depending on the sea-son, but to counter this, the family serves a *mechoui* or grillade of lamb on the roof terrace accompanied by traditional music during the sum-mer months. All rooms have air-conditioning.

➕ 181 E3 ✉ 30 rue Ali Belhouane ☎ 72 280818; fax: 72 282365

Bel Azur £££

The large Moorish-style Bel Azur, with its beautifully landscaped gar-dens, is just over 1km north of the town centre. Attractively positioned on a small headland and right next to a lovely sandy beach, the hotel is well known for its comprehensive evening entertainment which includes traditional Tunisian cul-tural shows, snake charmers and a fashionable nightclub.

➕ 181 E3 ✉ avenue Assad ibn el Fourat ☎ 72 280544; fax: 72 280275; email: belazurhotels@orangers.com.tn

Dar Hayet £££

One of Hammamet's many luxury hotels, but its advantage over the others is its relatively close proxim-ity to the town centre. A small hotel by Hammamet standards, the main building is based on a traditional Tunisian courtyard villa. All of the guest rooms are tastefully decorated and have air-conditioning and satellite television. Other facilities include a Moorish café and a pool surrounded by exceptionally beautiful landscaping.

181 E3 ✉ **rue Aqaba, Hammamet Beach** ☎ **72 282856; fax: 72 283399**

ÎLES KERKENNAH

Le Grand ££

The Grand is the best hotel in the Kerkennah Islands. Its excellent facilities include tennis courts, a swimming pool, two good restaurants and a bar. The hotel is usually booked in the high season, but it should be possible to get accommodation at other times of the year.

181 F1 ✉ **800m east of Remla bus stop** ☎ **74 281266; fax: 74 281485**

MAHDIA

Mahdia Palace Tryp £££

The Palace is the largest and most distinguished hotel in Mahdia. With comfortable, well-appointed rooms, good restaurants, a swimming pool, a variety of watersports and children's entertainment, it's a very good place to take a beach holiday.

181 E2 ✉ **route Touristique** ☎ **73 696777; fax: 73 696810**

Médina £

This converted médina house right in the centre of the old town provides simple, friendly, no-frills service, with breakfast included in the price.

181 E2 ✉ **Off rue Ali Bey, Médina** ☎ **73 694664**

MONASTIR

Club de l'Esplanade £££

Just south of the ribat or fortified monastery, close by the marina, the Club de l'Esplanade offers every conceivable facility from watersports to tennis, fine dining to very comfortable, well-appointed rooms.

181 E2 ✉ **route de la Corniche** ☎ **73 461146; fax: 73 460050**

establishment with a foyer fountain. Rooms are air-conditioned and have all the facilities that visitors would expect in a gracefully appointed hotel such as this. It's ideally placed for discovering the historic old town, and has parking facilities and a garden at the back.

181 E1 ✉ **boulevard des Martyrs,** ☎ **74 400700; fax: 74 405522**

SOUSSE

Médina ££

A wonderfully atmospheric location next to Sousse's Great Mosque, and if you don't mind being awoken by the muezzin's call to prayer, the Médina is a fine choice of lodgings. The spotlessly clean rooms all have en suite bathrooms. It's a very popular place in the summer with tour groups, so it's worth trying to book a room in advance. Unusually, for a hotel so close to a mosque, there's a bar.

181 E2 ✉ **15 rue Othman Osman** ☎ **73 221722; fax: 73 221794**

PORT EL KANTAOUI

Imperial Marhaba £££

With 232 rooms and 30 suites the Imperial Marhaba is one of the best hotels in Tunisia. From the huge marble entrance hall to the enormous outdoor swimming pool the hotel exudes class. Other facilities include an indoor swimming pool, fitness centre, hammam (Turkish bath), Tunisian-style coffee shop, tennis courts and a children's pool and playground. Many types of watersports are available between May and October.

181 E2 ✉ **3km north of the Port el Kantaoui marina** ☎ **73 246477; fax: 73 246377; www.imperialmarhaba.com**

SFAX

Hôtel des Arcades ££

At Sfax el-Jadida (New Sfax), near the northwestern corner of the old town, this is a comfortable and attractively decorated modern

Where to...
Eat and Drink

Prices

Expect to pay per person for a standard three-course meal, excluding drinks and service charges

£ under TD15   **££** TD15–TD30   **£££** over TD30DT

HAMMAMET

Barberousse ££

This restaurant is very popular in the summer months with a roof terrace offering pleasing views across the *médina*. Both international (with the emphasis on Italian) and local Tunisian cuisine are available, as well as a number of travellers' standbys such as fish and chips, steak and fried chicken. Alcohol is served.

🚹 181 E3 ⊠ Inside the *médina* ☎ 72 282037 ⓖ Daily 10:00 am–10:30 pm

Dar Lella ££

This is a long-established restaurant with a good reputation that draws in both locals and visitors. House specialities are Tunisian, especially *couscous*, deep fried chicken and a selection of tasty *mezze* (Arab hors-d'oeuvres). Service is friendly and courteous.

🚹 181 E3 ⊠ rue Patrice Lumumba ☎ 72 280871 ⓖ Daily 11–2, 5:30–11

La Médina ££

Located in the square by the *kasbah*, a major attraction of this consistently good restaurant is that the seating is on the ramparts of the *médina*. The usual combination of Tunisian and international food is on offer. Seafood is a house speciality; try the excellent *spaghetti aux fruits de mer* (seafood spaghetti).

🚹 181 E3 ⊠ Between the *kasbah* and place 7 Novembre ☎ 72 281728 ⓖ Daily 11–2:30, 5–10:30

La Scala £££

One of Hammamet's better Italian places, this intimate restaurant is located on a side road off the avenue des Nations Unies. Based on La Scala Opera House in Milan, the food is excellent and the location popular, so it's advisable to book in advance.

🚹 181 E3 ⊠ avenue des Nations Unies ☎ 72 287168 ⓖ Daily 11:30–2:30, 6–11; closed winter

Les Trois Moutons £££

Les Trois Moutons is generally reckoned to be one of the top restaurants in Tunisia, and certainly in Hammamet. There's an extensive *à la carte* menu specialising in seafood and meat dishes, as well as a good value set dinner on offer nightly. A fine wine list and a friendly ambience mean that the place is usually busy.

🚹 181 E3 ⊠ Centre Commercial, avenue Habib Bourguiba ☎ 72 280981 ⓖ Daily 11:30–2:30, 6–11

Restaurant Achour £££

Hidden away in a side street, this restaurant has an excellent reputation which draws in plenty of locals as well as visitors. It specialises in fish and seafood dishes; try the *loup de mer* (sea perch). It's a fashionable, up-market place, and consequently not cheap.

🚹 181 E3 ⊠ rue Ali Belhouane, ☎ 72 280140 ⓖ Daily 11–2:30, 6–11:30

ÎLES KERKENNAH

Cercina ££

Generally reckoned to be the best restaurant on the north side of

Chergui Island, seafood is the house speciality and the most popular dish is *tchich*, a thick and spicy octopus soup. A selection of wines and cold beer is available.

➕ 181 F1 ☒ Sidi Frej, 8km from Remla, Chergui Island ☎ 74 489953 ◉ Daily 11–2.30, 5.30–11

Restaurant de la Sirène ££
This modest restaurant on Chergui, the largest of the islands, offers an agreeable terrace, fresh fish, fried chicken, and beer and wine.

➕ 181 F1 ☒ Remla ☎ 74 481118 ◉ Daily lunch and dinner

KELIBIA

Pension Anis ££
An unusual restaurant, the Anis offers not just Tunisian and French dishes, but specialises in Franco-Tunisian "fusion seafood". Alcohol is served and the ambience is very agreeable.

➕ 181 E3 ☒ avenue Erriadh ☎ 72 295777 ◉ Daily 11–2.30, 6–11

Sidi el-Bahri £
This is a simple but very pleasant café overlooking Kelibia's harbour beneath the looming Byzantine castle. Here you can sit with a tea or coffee and watch the fishermen at their work.

➕ 181 E3 ☒ On the beach by the port ◉ Daily 7 am–7.30 pm

MAHDIA

Le Lido ££
A choice of *à la carte* and three-course set meals, overlooking the port. Wine and beer is served, and fresh seafood is the house speciality, with the fish *couscous* highly recommended.

➕ 181 E2 ☒ boulevard Farhat Hached ☎ 73 681339 ◉ Daily 11–2.30, 6–11

MONASTIR

Le King's ££
Good maritime views accompanied by fine Franco-Tunisian cuisine.

Aimed primarily at the tourist market, the quality is good enough to draw in plenty of locals as well.

➕ 181 E2 ☒ route de la Corniche ☎ 73 681867 ◉ Daily 10:30–2, 5–11

The Captain £££
For even more attractive views, this restaurant on the marina quay serves international food with some good fish, fried chicken and a variety of *couscous* dishes.

➕ 181 E2 ☒ Marina Quay ☎ 73 461449; fax: 73 473820 ◉ Daily 11–2.30, 6–11

PORT EL KANTAOUI

Daurade £££
Port el Kantaoui does not have cheap restaurants. Instead it has a selection of quite expensive ones, and the Daurade is one of the best. The restaurant serves both French and Tunisian cuisine.

➕ 181 E2 ☒ route de la Corniche ☎ 73 244893 ◉ Daily 12–2.30, 5.30–11:30

SFAX

Le Corail £££
Billed locally as the best restaurant in town, this tastefully decorated restaurant has a wide range of *à la carte* dishes, as well as an array of delicious salads and serves chilled beers and wines.

➕ 181 E1 ☒ 39 rue Habib Mazoun ☎ 74 227301 ◉ Daily 11:30–2, 5:30–11

SOUSSE

Le Lido £££
Le Lido, down by the harbour, is reputed to be Sousse's best restaurant, popular with locals and visitors alike. The extensive menu features many great fresh fish dishes, try the fish *tagine* or the lobster thermidor which, together with a good wine list, should satisfy most people's tastes.

➕ 181 E2 ☒ avenue Mohammed V ☎ 73 225329 ◉ Daily 11–2.30, 5:30–11

Where to... Shop

CERAMICS

Nabeul is justly famous as a pottery centre, and there are numerous shops selling the local ceramic wares. Try **Céramique Slama** at 190 avenue Farhat Hached, also the official **ONAT/SOCOPA** shop on avenue Thameur, the main Hammamet-Kelibia road, at the edge of the main *souq*. Other recommended outlets include **Société Socen** on avenue Habib Thameur (tel: 72 272200) and **Société Kerkeni**, also on avenue Habib Thameur (tel: 72 221808).

The vast pottery industry of Nabeul includes just about everything you can imagine, pots and dishes, flower pots, tiles and jugs, all covered with exuberant decoration, including the use of lead glazing introduced by a flood of Andalucian Muslim exiles from Spain in the 17th century. On Fridays there is a **camel market** in Nabeul – you may not wish to buy one of these large and cantankerous beasts, but it's quite a show.

SOUQS

The *souq* at **Hammamet** is a good place to shop for local souvenirs, but since the whole scene is very commercialised and aimed at overseas visitors, it's not the best place to look for bargains, unless you are an exceptionally capable and persistent shopper. The area near the *kasbah* and beach is the most tourist orientated part.

In **Sousse** town centre, best reached via the rue d'Angleterre, there are several *souqs* or marketplaces, some of them covered alleys with all sorts of intriguing objects on sale, including carpets and a lot of gold and other jewellery. Occasional attractive cafés allow you to withdraw from the throng and relax a while, but even here someone will generally try to attract your attention to a shop nearby. In **Souq al-Caid** and **Souq el-Reba** in the centre of the Sousse *médina* you will find much the same goods as in the more modern shopping centres. Souq el-Reba in particular is filled with perfumes, textiles, and jewellery. It is all aimed at the tourist, no doubt, but it is still great fun to wander around and explore these ancient market streets. In fact, in both **Sousse** and **Monastir**, even if you wander into smaller and more humble market streets, it is all but impossible to escape souvenirs aimed at tourists. This means prices are inevitably on the high side, except perhaps in the gold *souq* where everything depends on weight and locals, too, are intent on buying.

SHOPPING CENTRES

The large **Soula Shopping Centre** in **Sousse**, just north of the Great Mosque in the place Sidi Yahia, caters for visitors who want to buy quite large objects to be sent home. Olive wood carvings, jewellery, glass, pottery, leatherwork, cushions, carpets and rugs, even furniture, can all be found here on four floors; credit cards accepted.

In **Monastir** the similar **Yasmina Center** is located on rue Sakka, Houmt Chraka. Monastir also has the usual fixed-price **ONAT** shop, while Sousse has a **SOCOPA** outlet in the Hotel Abou Nawas Bou Jaafar.

ANTIQUES

In **Mahdia**, between the city gate and the place du Caire, there are a few interesting shops selling antiques, or at least old and attractive things. It is well worth taking a look.

Where to...
Be Entertained

NIGHTLIFE

The most active Western-style nightlife can be found in the large all-inclusive resorts at Hammamet and elsewhere in the Cap Bon Peninsula. In this category recommended venues include the **Tropicana Club** at the Hotel Hammamet Regency (tel: 72 226776) and the **Boule d'Argent** at the Hotel les Charmes (tel: 72 280016).

Elsewhere in **Hammamet** you should head out to the western part of town around avenue Moncef Bey. Here there are a number of lively local clubs, notably the **Discothèque Manhattan** (tel: 72 226226) which has a laser show and the Elysée Restaurant with

"animation orientale" – in actual fact a Tunisian band. A similar venue on avenue Moncef Bey is **Le Calypso** (tel: 72 00216). For a quiet drink where you can meet the locals, the **Café-Bar le Palmier** on avenue de la République is perhaps the best-appointed and most friendly bar in town.

North of **Sousse** town centre, the **Maracana** at the Hotel Tej Marhaba (tel: 73 229800) and the nearby **Samara** at the Samara Hotel (tel: 73 226699) are the best local nightclubs, though there are others in some of the big hotels. If you're in the mood for a flutter, check out the **Casino Caraïbe** on boulevard 7 Novembre (tel: 73 211777).

In **Mahdia** the local hotspot is the **Samba** nightclub in Hotel El

Mehdi on route de la Corniche (tel: 73 671287).

Tunisia's second largest city, **Sfax** isn't really a tourist destination, and this is reflected in the nightlife which is aimed chiefly at locals. The **Restaurant Alexander** at the Hotel Alexander, 21 rue Alexandre Dumas (tel: 74 221613) offers a folk music show every Saturday evening. By late in the evening it can get pretty raucous, but it's a lot of fun.

SPORT

There are a number of good golf courses around Hammamet, notably **Yasmine** (tel: 72 227001; fax: 72 226722), and **Citrus** (tel: 72 226500; fax: 72 226400), both of which have good 18-hole courses. At Port el Kantaoui there is a large 27-hole course, **Golf El-Kantaoui** (tel: 73 231755) and at Skanès an 18-hole course, **Palm Links** (tel: 73 466910; fax: 73 466913). For sailing, fishing and diving and other

watersports try **Cap Monastir Underwater Diving Centre**, (tel: 73 461156) and at Port el Kantaoui, Port de Plaisance, the **International Diving Centre** (tel: 73 241799).

FESTIVALS

On the Cap Bon Peninsula festivals are held to celebrate special local events. In June there is a **Falconry Festival** at El Haouaria, a **Wine Festival** at Grombalia, and an annual **International Cultural Festival** at the Centre International Culturel, Hammamet, in the former house of Georges Sebastian, during July and August. There's also the **Sousse International Festival**, and at El Jem the **International Festival of Symphonic Music**, both held annually, the first in July and August, the second in July in the great El Jem amphitheatre. You can get programmes from the local Tourism Offices (▶ 35).

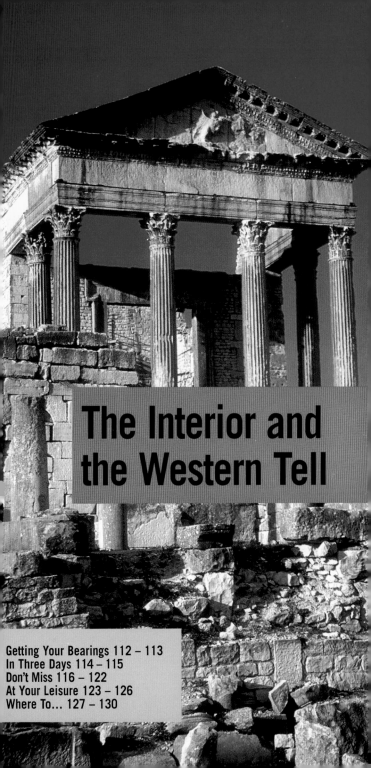

The Interior and the Western Tell

Getting Your Bearings

The interior and the western hill country of Tunisia is a large and varied area, lying south of the Mejerda river valley. It is largely mountainous but as you progress southwards the land becomes more arid, fading into the region of the desert and mountain oases, then the salt lakes, or *chotts*, on the edge of the Sahara.

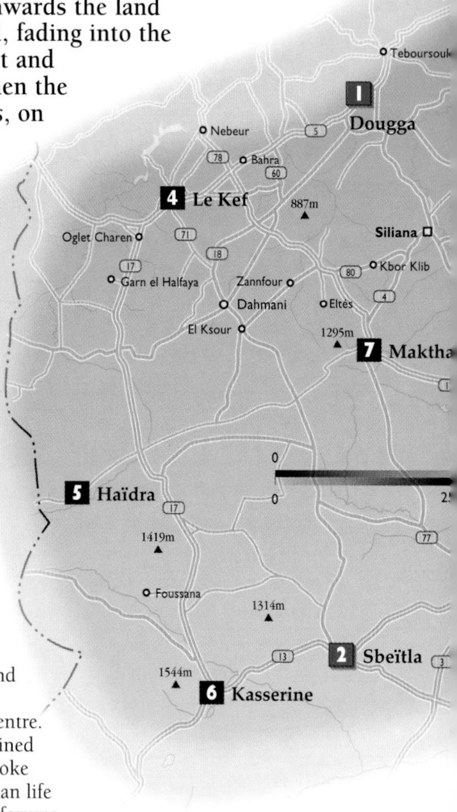

To the east is the flatter land leading to the coast, with Kairouan as the chief town. Indeed Kairouan is Tunisia's holiest city and is revered throughout the Islamic world. It is famed for its ancient and exquisite mosque, the most prominent in all North Africa, its delightful *médina* rich in architectural attractions, and its colourful carpet industry.

This is also a region where Roman cities abound, from Dougga and Thuburbo Majus in the north to Sbeïtla in the centre. These towns are now ruined but still splendid and evoke nostalgic images of Roman life 2,000 years ago in their forums, amphitheatres and baths.

Tunisia's interior is an area where you can leave your hotel and swimming pool behind and get out and explore. Even those who have little interest in history will be amazed by the ruins at Dougga and Sbeïtla.

You might want to carry your walking boots, as this is a popular area for hiking and there is always the prospect of Tunisia's highest mountain, the 1,544m-high Jebel Chambi.

o Teboursouk

1 Dougga

o Nebeur ⑤

78 o Bahra
60

4 Le Kef   887m ▲

Oglet Charen o   71   **Siliana** □

18   80 o Kbor Klib

o Garn el Halfaya   Zannfour o   ④

o Dahmani   oEltès

El Ksour o   1295m ▲

7 Maktha

5 Haïdra

17   77

1419m ▲

o Foussana   1314m ▲

1544m ▲   13   **2** Sbeïtla

6 Kasserine

0

0   2.

Previous page: The substantial remains surrounding the Capitol at Dougga

TUNIS

36

8 Zaghouan

9 Thuburbo Majus

988m

Oum El Abouab   Ouled Abdallah

Bir Chaouach

Ouled Ameur

El Jema   Koundar

Sbikha   El Alam

816m

ula

El Batlen   **3** Kairouan

Cherichira   Regueda

Fondoul Loussaïef   66

Menzel Mehiri

Nasr Allah

An avenue of eucalyptus trees cast their shadows over the road to Tunis near Kairouan

Below: Beautiful late afternoon light bathes the fields around Dougga

Enjoy grand Roman cities, fascinating mosques and precarious cliff fortresses on this tour of Tunisia's dusty and mountainous interior.

The Interior and the Western Tell in Three Days

Day One

Morning
Starting from Tunis head westwards on Autoroute 5 for about 100km to the town of Teboursouk. You should buy last-minute provisions (including plenty of water) here before you head off to the Roman ruins of Dougga.

Afternoon
Prepare to be impressed and to spend at least three hours at ❶ **Dougga** (➤ 116). Enjoy a picnic and linger for a while to appreciate the extent of the civilisation that the Romans created here. Continue on Autoroute 5 towards ❹ **Le Kef** (below, ➤ 123).

Evening
Stay overnight at Le Kef and dine at Chez Venus (➤ 128). Take a look at the shrine at Ain el-Kef in the town centre.

Day Two

Morning
Climb up to the twin fortresses or *kasbah* on the cliff overlooking the city. Visit the Musée Régional des Arts et Traditions Populaires to get a grounding on the local Berber culture and traditions.

Afternoon
Proceed southwards about 120km to ❻ **Kasserine** (Mausoleum of Flavius Secondus and Petrouan, right; ➤ 125) and then to ❷ **Sbeïtla** (➤ 118). You can take lunch opposite the magnificent Roman ruins here. For more Roman ruins head north through the forests and gorges to ❼ **Makthar** (➤ 125) before continuing eastwards on to Kairouan.

Evening

In **3 Kairouan** (belts on display, above; ➤ 120) take a stroll around the fascinating labyrinth of the *médina*. For a fine dinner, Fairouz (➤ 128) on avenue Habib Bourguiba is recommended.

Day Three

Morning

Kairouan deserves time to explore the many great sites. Be sure to visit the Grande Mosquée de Sidi Oqba, one of the most famous mosques in the world. A multi-site ticket will give you entry to seven of the top attractions. However, if you have spent the last days rummaging around Roman ruins you might want a morning to relax, so enjoy a long, luxurious *hammam* bath in the *médina*.

Afternoon/Evening

Have lunch in the *médina* before you set off back to Tunis, about 150km away. You can either take Autoroute 2 which leads to Hammamet (➤ 102) via the coast road, or you can drive straight north on Autoroute 3 and make a small diversion to **8 Zaghouan** (➤ 126). You'll pass the splendid remains of the Roman Zaghouan–Carthage aqueduct. If you have time, climb the hill to visit the Temple des Eaux. A local legend states that if you drink the water here you will always return to Tunisia.

1 Dougga

Dougga, a UNESCO World Heritage site, is the largest, the most spectacular and the best-preserved of all the Roman towns of Tunisia. Here you can walk along roads rutted by the wheels of supply carts, and wander through the ancient forum, markets, colonnades, pillars, temples, baths and private villas. With a little imagination you can reconstruct a good impression of life in a city of the Roman Empire nearly 2,000 years ago

Dougga lies southwest of Tunis near the town of Teboursouk. Approaching from the north via Djebba and Teboursouk there are wonderful views from below the rock face and over the hills framing the Mejerda valley. The Roman colonialists built this impressive town on the site of the ancient Carthaginian town of Thugga, which was at one time the seat of Massinissa, King of Numidia (➤ 8).

Roman Emperor Septimius Severus (AD 193–211) declared Dougga a *municipium* (free town), and a triumphal arch was erected in AD 205 to celebrate this. Another triumphal arch was built to honour the town's privileges by Alexander Severus (AD 222–235), and this arch, more or less intact, is still one of the town's most imposing remains.

The magnificent **Capitol**, completed in AD 166, bears a sculpted figure of Emperor Antoninus Pius (AD 138–61) on the pediment, and has been meticulously restored with its tall columns and 10m-high stone walls. Beside it is the **forum**, with its portico and columns, which was partly destroyed by the Byzantine commander Solomon when he constructed a fortified enclosure here.

The **theatre**, still in excellent condition, was sliced out of the rock of the hillside. Designed to accommodate 3,500 people, it is still used for plays and concerts in the summer months. An important temple was dedicated to the Carthaginian deity, Baal Hamon and

Above: The portico of the 3rd century AD Temple of Juno

Below: Dougga remains one of the most striking ruined cities in the Mediterranean

in AD 195 a **Temple of Saturn** was built over this. Two foot-prints carved into the paving are said to represent a visit by the god Saturn to his sanctuary. The **Plaza of the Winds** was once a market place. It was so named because there is a wind indicator inscribed with the names of the twelve winds carved into its paving.

The **Baths of Licinius**, built in the 3rd century AD, still survive in fairly good condition, with their different hot and cold rooms and heating system. The *palaestra* or gymnasium is next door, and in the street leading to the baths is the **House of the Cup-Bearers**, named after the mosaic that was found here, which like many other mosaics from Dougga is now housed at the Musée du Bardo (► 60) in Tunis.

TAKING A BREAK

There is a small café beside the theatre which sells basic snacks, but Dougga is the perfect place to **enjoy a picnic**. Take your choice from the many picturesque spots around the site.

🚩 180 C3
✉ 110km southwest of Tunis on Autoroute 5
🕐 Daily 7–7 (8:30–5:30 in winter)

🚌 Hourly daytime services from Tunis to Le Kef which stop at Nouvelle Dougga, 3km from the site
🎫 Inexpensive

DOUGGA: INSIDE INFO

Top tips Allow at least **three hours** to fully appreciate the ruins.
• **Arrive early** to avoid crowds and the heat.
• You should come prepared with **walking shoes, a hat, sunblock and water**; there's not much shade to be found.

② Sbeïtla

In this rather desolate region of the Western Tell it may seem strange to find Roman cities on the scale of Sbeïtla. But at one time this region was richly forested and olive trees grew in abundance, making olive oil the cash crop of the Roman colonialists. Sbeïtla was the most southerly of the Roman cites and is second only to Dougga in Tunisia for the monumental nature of its ruins. Today the site is preserved as an archaeological park, with a complex of shops and cafés.

A large Roman triumphal arch, called locally the **Bab Sbeïtla** (Gate of Sbeïtla), stands at the entrance to the ruins. Further towards the town, you can observe two relatively well-preserved Byzantine guard posts. Byzantine fortification attests to the frontier nature of the town and its battles with unsubdued Berber peoples to the south. The main street is paved and you'll find the **Church of Severus** near by; it was named after an inscription commemorating a priest of that name.

The **forum** is still rather splendid, with, unusually, three (roofless but largely intact) temples of the Capitoline triad: Minerva, Jupiter and Juno. They stand on a plinth reached by two staircases. The forum was built in AD 139, the period of the city's

The remains of the temples dedicated to Minerva, Jupiter and Juno

zenith. In front stands a monumental gate constructed by Emperor Antoninus Pius. You can visit a large cistern, as well as the impressive **public baths**, one of five separate bathing complexes discovered so far. The baths are well preserved, with pools and basins, mosaics and an under-floor heating system or hypocaust. Below them on the hill is the **theatre**, with some of the columns of the stage still standing in front of damaged rows of seating. There is also a ruined amphitheatre close by.

During the Byzantine period an ecclesiastical complex was built, consisting of the **basilicas** of St. Vitalis (a Christian soldier martyred near Geneva in AD 286) and Bellator (a bishop whose name was found on an inscription here). The choir of the Bellator church is decorated with attractive mosaics. The church still has its columned baptistery with font, which later became the chapel of Bishop Jucundus. The ruins date from the 6th century and lie behind the forum to the north. The church of Vitalis was much larger, and its form is still easy to make out.

A crudely carved representation of a Roman nobleman

TAKING A BREAK

Opposite the site the restaurant **La Capitole** (➤ 128) makes a good break from the heat; the upstairs section serves food and downstairs in the courtyard drinks are available.

✚ 180 C1
✉ 117km west of Kairouan on Autoroute 3
🕐 Daily 7–7 (8:30–5:30 in winter)
🚌 Three buses daily from Kairouan
💷 Moderate

SBEÏTLA: INSIDE INFO

Top tip If you are visiting Sbeïtla in the evening or in the winter **wear warm clothing**. The ruins lies at an altitude of over 1,000m and the night air can be chilly.

In more detail The local museum exhibits a few mosaics and other objects, including some little **funerary stelae** from the graveyards carved with figures of the deceased. However, the best mosaics have been moved to the Musée du Bardo (➤ 60) in Tunis.

3 Kairouan

Many lands have a "holy city" which outranks all others for local religious sentiment. Kairouan is Tunisia's. It's regarded as Islam's fourth most sacred city, after Jerusalem, Medina and Mecca. As a centre of pilgrimage and prayer, the *médina* alone boasts no less than 50 mosques within its walls.

Kairouan lies on the route through the arid steppe region which was once travelled by caravans of camels that crossed the Sahara from the south towards Tunis. It was here that Uqba ibn Nafi camped and plotted the Arab conquest of North Africa in AD 670. Known as Al-Qayrawan, the city prospered after it was selected as capital by the Aghlabid ruler c800, and remained a political centre under Fatimid and Zirid successors.

Inside the *Médina*

The old *médina* is in the shape of an irregular oblong surrounded by 7km of walls and ramparts and covers some 30ha. It is fascinating to walk around this bustling area, which includes markets for livestock, grain and handicraft products. An estimated 12,000 families are engaged in carpet manufacture and you can expect some aggressive sales techniques.

Crossing the city east–west is avenue Habib Bourguiba, from the Bab el-Tunis (Tunis Gate) to the Bab el-Chouhada (Martyrs' Gate), and north of here are the *souqs*. Inside the Bab el-Chouhada on a street to the right is the 14th-century **Zaouia Sidi Abid el-Ghariani** (Mausoleum of Sidi Abid el-Ghariani), an elaborately decorated shrine which is now open

Kairouan's 17th-century covered *souq* is full of bargains

to non-Muslims since the Sufi holy man's remains have been transferred elsewhere.

Further in towards the heart of the *médina* is the **Mosquée el Bey** (Bey's Mosque) and **Bir Barouta** (Barouta's Well), supposedly named after Sidi Oqba's dog, who originally discovered the well. Here, an unfortunate blindfolded camel turns a wheel that pumps up water said to be holy since it derives from Mecca.

Moving north in the *médina* you will find the 9th-century **Mosquée des Trois Portes** (Mosque of the Three Doors), with a very attractive façade carved with Arabic texts. The three doors in question are separate entrances for men, women and children.

The Grande Mosquée de Sidi Oqba (The Great Mosque)

In the north corner of the old city is the Great Mosque founded by Uqba ibn Nafi in AD 671, though its present form is predominantly a 9th-century structure from Aghlabid times.

The mosque is an impressive building, stately and graceful with its court, its mighty cedar doors under horseshoe-shaped stone arches, and particularly its huge 400-pillar prayer hall. Many of the columns are of different colours and types of stones, and were taken from the Roman ruins at El Jem and Carthage. Entry to the prayer hall is forbidden to non-Muslims, but through the open doors you can glimpse the lovely interior, with its 9th-century *minbar* or pulpit, said to be the oldest surviving *minbar* in the world, decorated with 250 carved wooden panels. Outside you can inspect the massive 35m-high minaret rising in three stages, topped with a dome. There are 128 steps to the top which is capped with Christian tombstones.

The **Zaouia Sidi Sahab** houses the remains of Abu Azama al-Balawia, a companion of the prophet Muhammad. The mosque is sometimes called the "Barber's Mosque" because he wore a locket containing three hairs from Muhammad's beard. The elaborate tile work and attractive mosaics are 17th-century, but the graceful colonnades and the interior of the building are beautifully and richly ornamented in the classic Islamic geometric style.

Though Kairouan is the spiritual and religious capital of Tunisia, commerce is never far way; vividly coloured carpets outside a carpet showroom

TAKING A BREAK

The hotel restaurant of **La Kasbah** (➤ 128) specialises in buffets. Wine and beer are served and there is also a swimming pool where you can cool off.

Pilgrims converse at a doorway leading into the Zaouia Sidi Sahab

➕ 181 D2
⊠ 70km west of Sousse
🚍 Regular service between Tunis and the south
⊠ avenue de la République, multi-site ticket provides entry to most of the city's major attractions
🎟 Moderate

Grande Mosquée de Sidi Oqba
⊠ boulevard Ibrahim ibn Aghlab, with the main gate on boulevard Brahim ben Lagheb
🕐 Sat–Thu 7:30–2 (8–2:30 in winter), Fri 8–12

Zaouia Sidi Sahab
⊠ avenue de la République
🕐 Daily 8:30–5:30

Mosquée el Bey
⊠ avenue Ali Belhouane
🕐 Daily 8–5:30

Mosquée des Trois Portes
⊠ rue de la Mosquée des Trois Portes
🕐 Daily 8–4

Zaouia Sidi Abid el-Ghariani
⊠ rue Sidi el-Ghariani
🕐 Sat–Thu 8:30–1, 3–6 (closed Friday afternoon)

Bassins des Aghlabides
⊠ avenue de la République
🕐 Daily 8–12, 3–7 (8:30–5:30 in winter)

KAIROUAN: INSIDE INFO

Top tips The Office de Tourisme, place des Bassins des Aghlabides, sells **multi-site tickets** which cover seven of the major city sights.

• From the roof of the Office de Tourisme there is an excellent bird's-eye view over the **Bassins des Aghlabides** (Aghlabid Basins), part of the sophisticated waterworks that served the city in the 9th century. Water was brought in from the Tell some 35km away.

At Your Leisure

🄳 Le Kef

Le Kef ("The Cliff") sits on a 780m-high outcrop of Jebel Dyr, part of the High Tell region of Tunisia. It's the country's most important inland city after Kairouan.

tant stronghold here. It also provided a haven to the Libres Françaises (Free French) resistance in World War II.

Today the remains of the past greatly enhance the town, with pow-

The old Turkish fort looms over Le Kef

The Carthaginians built a fortress here, but they were not the first settlers, as ancient stone tools from the region show. The presence of a source of water at **Ain el-Kef** was certainly important, and there may have been a sacred element to the spring. A shrine here to Lalla Ma, Lady of the Waters, still attracts devotion, as it has for centuries. There are cafés and a garden in the hollow where the spring rises. You can also see the original Roman stonework.

Le Kef retained a certain importance to the Romans: it was near here, at Zama, that they defeated Hannibal. The Byzantine period saw the construction of a church and later the Turks maintained an impor-

erful walls and towers, and a few old cannons. Two dominating forts or **kasbahs**, joined by a drawbridge, are seated firmly on the cliff. The first and largest is of Byzantine origin, while the second was built in the 18th century.

From the fort you can look down into the columned courtyards of two substantial stone buildings below. One is the **Jemaa el Kebir**, or Great Mosque, one of the country's oldest buildings, dating back to the 4th century. The other is the 17th-century **Mosquée de Sidi Bou Makhluf**, named after the patron saint of Le Kef. His mosque is elegant in its pure whiteness, with a fine octagonal minaret decorated with rich tiling. Le Kef has a total of nine *zaouia* (mausoleums), and one, the Sidi Ali Ben Aissa, now houses the **Musée Régional des Arts et Traditions Populaires** (Regional Museum of Popular Arts and Traditions) which is worth visiting to learn more about the culture of the nomadic Berber people.

➕ 180 B3 ✉ 170km southwest of Tunis

Aïn el-Kef
✉ place de l'Indépendance (opposite Hotel Sicca Veneria) 🕐 Open access
🎫 Free

Kasbahs
✉ rue el-Kasbah 🕐 Tue–Sun 7–5
🎫 Free

Musée Régional des Arts et Traditions Populaires ✉ place Ben Aissa ☎ 78 221503 🕐 Tue–Sun 9–1, 4–7 (9:30–4:30 in winter)
🎫 Inexpensive

of one of Byzantium's largest fortresses in Africa represent an imperial might that dissolved before the advancing Arabs in the late 7th century. The ruins of no less than five churches are visible here too, witnesses to the conquest of Islam. Haïdra was occupied by Phoenicians and Romans, who created a settlement called Ammaedara, on the very frontiers of Roman Africa and the Numidian region. A triumphal arch, erected to Septimius Severus, the African Emperor, can be seen as you arrive at the site. Behind it, in a field, is a mausoleum built to resemble a temple, among the better-preserved monuments at this largely unexcavated site.

North of Haïdra is a huge, flat-topped, sheer-sided mountain, named Le Table de Jugurtha (Jugurtha's Table) after the Numidian king who defied Rome. The massive silhouette of the 1,271m-high mountain is clearly visible from the main road through Tajerouine south of Le

5 Haïdra

In this remote and desolate spot close to the Algerian border, the ruins of a Byzantine settlement surround an imposing fortress. The great round bastion and solid walls

Sheep graze below the ruins at Haïdra

Kef. For those with the stamina, the ascent is rewarding. Start from the village of Kalaat Es Senan; allow 2–3 hours and carry plenty of water.

⊞ 180 B2 ⊠ Halfway between Le Kef and Kasserine on Route 4 ◉ Open access ♨ Free

❻ Kasserine

Kasserine, a market town near the 1,544m-high Jebel Chambi mountain, is a favourite area for hikers and hunters. It is also an important junction for road and rail in this region of irrigated grain fields, olives, sheep and cattle-raising.

It was here that the Allied army lost so many men when opposing the German army in 1943 (► 21).

The name Kasserine means "Two Castles", referring to the Roman mausoleums that stand here. One, the monument to Flavius Secundus, is still well preserved. To the right as you leave the town heading southwards, you can't help but notice this towering structure.

⊞ 180 B1 ⊠ 40km southwest of Sbeïtla on Autoroute 13, 110km south of Le Kef on Autoroute 17

❼ Makthar

Makthar is situated on a high plateau amid some of the most beautiful scenery in the country. This small town of 8,000 people is surrounded by gorges and forests, and lies 17km beyond the interesting Berber hillside village of Kesra on the road from Kairouan.

In Roman times it was called Mactaris, a town they conquered from its Numidian rulers in 46 BC. It became prosperous in the 2nd century, but suffered much in later centuries as Vandals, Byzantines and Arabs assaulted it in turn.

The well-preserved colonnade surrounding the *schola juvenum* at Makthar

An amphitheatre, a forum and a triumphal arch dedicated to Emperor Trajan are among the surviving ruins. The 2nd-century baths, with wave-patterned mosaics, were so commanding in size that they were incorporated into a Byzantine fortress. A paved road to the baths leads past the ruins of a church named after a man of Vandal ancestry called Hildegun, who was buried at the entrance. A temple of Bacchus stands opposite the old forum, and there is also a *schola juvenum* or

A Berber woman harvesting wheat

meeting place for young men, now a tree-shaded ruin that was partly converted into a church. Just inside the entrance to the site is a modest museum with displays of Punic, Roman and Christian objects.

➕ 180 C2 ✉ 115km west of Kairouan on Autoroute 12, halfway to Le Kef ☎ 78 787651 ⏰ Daily 8–6 (8:30–5:30 in winter) 🎟 Inexpensive

8 Zaghouan

This small but picturesque town of some 10,000 people lies on the fertile north side of the impressive jagged peaks of the 1,295m-high Mount Zaghouan.

This was the old Roman site of Zigus, from where a 70km-long aqueduct and canal network brought fresh water to Roman Carthage. Parts of it can still be seen along the route to Tunis.

In AD 130, to honour the nymph of the local source, Emperor Hadrian had a Temple des Eaux (Temple of the Waters) built. The structure has an unusual point of interest: a row of 12 niches built in a semicircular bay above a basin which collects water. The niches once held statues emblematic of the 12 Roman months. A local proverb claims that whoever drinks Zaghouan water will always return to Tunisia. Situated on a hill, it is today the most impressive sight in the town.

The Temple des Eaux at Zaghouan

➕ 181 D3 ✉ 60km south of Tunis, 30km west of Hammamet ⏰ Open access 🎟 Free

9 Thuburbo Majus

Pink-veined marble columns greet visitors today at the Roman baths in Thuburbo Majus. The town was originally a Carthaginian settlement, and probably a Berber one before that, established in a shallow valley between the hills. By Emperor Hadrian's reign it had become an important regional agricultural market, until damaged by the Vandal invasion in 407.

The site itself is impressive, with walls, plinths and some of the columns still standing. In the centre is the rather battered forum surrounded by colonnades and shops. The Capitoline temple, built in AD 168, is one of Africa's largest temples with its four massive pillars. Parts of the colossal 7m-high statue of Jupiter are now in the Musée du Bardo (▶ 60) in Tunis. The Winter Baths were built further up the hill, one of five bathing complexes at Thuburbo Majus. You should also have a look at the Palaestra Petronii which was once a gymnasium

➕ 181 D3 ✉ 60km southwest of Tunis on Autoroute 3 ⏰ Daily 8–7 (8:30–5:30 in winter) 🎟 Inexpensive

Where to... Stay

Prices

Expect to pay for a standard double room per night
£ under TD50 ££ TD50–TD100 £££ over TD100DT

KAIROUAN

La Kasbah £££

This is the most luxurious hotel in Kairouan. Built in the massive old fort, it is very conveniently situated for walks into the *souqs* and to explore the monuments. Inside there is a beautiful arched lobby leading to comfortable rooms, some with small enclosed balconies and overlooking the heated swimming pool in the courtyard below. There's a good restaurant (often with buffet selection, since this is a hotel that caters for tour groups). There are less expensive hotels in Kairouan, but if you can splurge, this one is certainly the best place to choose.

✚ 181 D2 ⊠ avenue Ibn al-Jazzar
☎ 77 237301; fax: 77 237302; email:
kasbah.kairouan@gnet.tn

Sabra £

A very friendly establishment aimed squarely at budget travellers. All rooms have hot water and breakfast is included in the price. The helpful management can arrange sightseeing tours and other excursions. The hotel's roof terrace provides great views over the old *médina* and immediately next door there's a *hammam* where you can enjoy a vigorous Turkish massage and a good steam bath.

✚ 181 D2 ⊠ rue Ali Belhouane, Bab
es-Shouhada ☎ 77 230263

LE KEF

Résidence Vénus £

Perhaps the best place in town, although not the most expensive. Set in the old *kasbah*, this small, family-run establishment is clean, welcoming and provides a good breakfast. All rooms have private bathrooms and air-conditioning. Good value for money.

✚ 180 B3 ⊠ rue Mouldi Khamessi
☎ 78 204695

Sicca Veneria £

Situated in the middle of the town, near the spring of Ras al-Ain and its small lake and gardens, the Sicca Veneria is a spotlessly clean and comfortable hotel. The rooms have few amenities, but possess a certain charm. There is also a restaurant, the Salle Rose, and a lively bar frequented by the locals, which serves cold beer and local or imported wines and spirits.

✚ 180 B3 ⊠ place de
l'Indépendance ☎ 78 202389

SBEÏTLA

Sufetula ££

The best hotel in the vicinity of Sbeïtla, the Sufetula offers good views over the ancient ruins from its hillside location. All the large rooms are air-conditioned, but offer few other amenities. Full board is pretty much a necessity in this out-of-the-way place.

✚ 180 C1 ⊠ 1.5km north of Sbeïtla
on rue Kasserine ☎ 77 465074;
fax: 77 465582

TEBOURSOUK

Thugga ££

A fairly standard, modern hotel with little character, this is nevertheless the best place to stay close to the ruins at Dougga. Breakfast is included in the price and makes good sense for an early start to nearby Dougga. Half-board is available.

✚ 180 C3 ⊠ rue Tunis-Le Kef ☎ 78
466647; fax: 78 466721

Where to...
Eat and Drink

Prices

Expect to pay per person for a standard three-course meal, excluding drinks and service charges

£ under TD15   ££ TD15–TD30   £££ over TD30

KAIROUAN

La Kasbah ££

The hotel restaurant of La Kasbah specialises in buffet spreads, while the kitchen also supplies made-to-order local specialities. The chef prides himself on his local Tunisian dishes which tend to be spicier than usual, with lots of *harissa* pepper sauce an important ingredient. Wine, cold beer and various imported spirits are served. The comfortable seating is in a good setting overlooking the large courtyard swimming pool.

🚹 181 D2 ✉ avenue Ibn al-Jazzar
☎ 77 237301; fax: 77 237302
🕐 Daily 11:30–2:00, 6–11:30

Roi de Couscous £

This basic but friendly Tunisian eating place specialises not only in varieties of *couscous*, but in snacks like pizza, spaghetti, spicy Tunisian-style macaroni and burgers with french fries. The restaurant bar offers cold beer and other alcohol, but most locals seem content to settle for hot mint tea.

🚹 181 D2 ✉ place du 7 Novembre
🕐 Daily 11:30–2, 5:30–10:30

Sabra £

Like the nearby Roi de Couscous, this local restaurant serves Tunisian specialities and various international dishes like steak and chips, grilled chicken and some excellent salads. There is a small *à la carte* menu supplemented by fixed, three-course meals. Sabra is a popular venue with the locals.

🚹 181 D2 ✉ avenue de la
République 🕐 Daily 10:30–1,
5:30–9.30

LE KEF

Chez Vénus ££

This establishment has something of a local café touch; it's centrally situated, and offers the best choice and quality of food in the town. There's a fixed-price set menu as well as an extensive *à la carte* selection including French, Italian and Tunisian dishes.

🚹 180 B3 ✉ rue Farhat Hached
☎ 78 204695 🕐 Daily 8:30–1.30,
5:30–11

Salle Rose £

The Salle Rose is a pleasant restaurant on the first floor in the Sicca Veneria hotel (▶ 127), serving good local and international dishes in an intimate setting. The lamb and beef kebabs are tender and very tasty, as is the chicken *couscous*. Also recommended is the Italian-style lasagne verdi. Salle Rose also offers a wider and more varied selection of vegetables than at many comparable Tunisian restaurants.

🚹 180 B3 ✉ place de
l'Indépendance ☎ 78 202389
🕐 Daily 11:30–2, 5:30–10.30

SBEITLA

La Capitole ££

Arriving at Sbeitla, you naturally head for the ruins in the park. Just opposite, in a large building that also houses the ticket office, is La Capitole. Here you can drink a cold beer and survey the ruins from above, or eat grilled meat, omelette and other dishes and recover your strength for the exploration of the site. There's a useful arcade with shops near by where you can buy cold water or chilled soft drinks to take to the park with you, as shade is very limited

🖽 180 C1 🖾 Opposite the ruin park, Sbeitla 🕾 77 466880 🕜 Daily 8:30–5:30

TEBOURSOUK

Thugga £

This is a very popular restaurant with locals as well as with visitors. Of course it helps that there are hardly any other restaurants to compete with them in the area, but nonetheless the menu is quite extensive and will satisfy just about anyone who visits. It includes local dishes such as *marcassin* or baby wild boar, pigeon when available and good fried chicken and chips. Cold beer and other alcoholic drinks are served.

🖽 180 C3 🖾 rue Tunis–Le Kef 🕾 78 466647 🕜 Daily 11:30–2:30, 6–11

Where to… Shop

Kairouan is the largest city of the Interior and the Western Tell and is therefore the best place to shop. Its *souqs* are full of interesting goods, from gold and silver to hand-woven blankets. Part of the fun is merely wandering and looking, but there are so many attentive touts to lure you to this or that shop that keeping on course is sometimes quite difficult. Outside the *medina* there is an **ONAT/SOCOPA** fixed prices are always somewhat higher than those in the market-place.

There's an **ONAT Carpet Museum**, also on avenue Ali Zouaoui, which is in fact a retail outlet for carpets as well as a genuine museum. Carpets are one of the chief products of the region, and the artisans of Kairouan produce fine examples of both woven *mergoum* and hand-knotted rugs.

Perhaps the best place to buy these is the **Centre des Traditions et des Metiers d'Art de Kairouan** on a narrow side street just north of Bir Barouta by the Souq el-Blaghija. This is yet another fixed-price place that was established by ONAT to promote local handicrafts. Sales are handled downstairs, while upstairs there are displays of traditional rug-making, embroidery and weaving.

Copper objects are another Kairouan speciality, as are sesame seed date cakes called *makhroud*. Look for both in the busy *souqs* at the heart of the old *medina*.

Le Kef also has its share of *souqs*, but the atmosphere and the goods for sale differ somewhat from Kairouan. **Jewellery** is a local speciality, and there are several interesting silver and gold shops just up the hill from the Ras el-Ain spring, by the place de l'Independance, right in the centre of the town. Popular items include interlocking gold chains of the type local brides wear, silver boxes and mirror frames with chased decoration; there are many other designs too.

If you want a special Tunisian souvenir associated particularly with this area, then enquire about the local tailors who dedicate themselves to making camel-hair hooded *burnus*. You'll see a lot of locals wearing these rather heavy garments in temperatures that might seem rather too hot for such thick clothing. Finally, if you're pining for a bottle of wine, head out to place Tahar ben Brahim in the southeastern part of town; here, unexpectedly, on the west side of the square is the city **wine shop**.

Teboursouk has little in the way of shopping besides some postcards. The same is true of **Sbeitla**, the main overnight stop for visitors to the ruins at Sufetula.

Where to...
Be Entertained

NIGHTLIFE

Nightlife in Tunisia's empty interior and Western Tell is, inevitably, rather limited. Visitors to this region will not be seeking discos or cabarets, rather life here is more *à la Tunisienne*, and this is part of the area's rather laid-back appeal. Relaxation here tends to revolve around long evenings conversing in local cafés, drinking sweet Turkish coffee rather than alcohol, and smoking the traditional *chicha* or "hubble bubble" water pipe, perhaps over a game of chequers or backgammon.

Kairouan is the region's largest town, but it's also Tunisia's holiest city, the location where Islam was first established in the Maghreb (Western North Africa) and as such rather conservative and even austere. Nevertheless, the **Hotel Amina** on the route de Tunis has a "nightclub" of sorts, with alcohol for sale and traditional local music and cultural shows. There's also a choice of attractive bars at **La Kasbah** (▲ 127), Kairouan's top hotel. More basic but quite friendly is the bar at **Le Splendid** on avenue 9 Avril 1939 (tel: 77 227522), but as it is popular with local drinkers it can be a bit noisy.

Le Kef is smaller than Kairouan and has still less to offer by way of nightlife, which is limited to a choice of beer, wine or local spirits at **Sicca Veneria** (▲ 127) on the place de l'Independance (tel: 78 221561). The same is true of **Sbeitla**, although the bar at the **Sufetula** (▲ 127) is much more attractive, though no more friendly, than at Le Kef; less appealing and more anonymous is the simply-named **Bar/Restaurant** on avenue Habib Bourguiba. More bar than restaurant, this is another place to stop for a sundowner or nightcap in this otherwise teetotal backwater.

BATHING

Bathing may seem an unusual pursuit in the midst of the Tunisian desert, but at **Hammam Mellegue**, 15km west of Le Kef, visitors have a unique opportunity to indulge in an authentic Roman bath. The baths, which date from the 2nd century AD, are at the foot of a dramatic escarpment overlooking the Oued Mellegue. After 1800 years the *caldarium* or hot room remains unchanged and still in use. Stone steps lead down to a bathing pool fed by natural hot springs in a subterranean chamber. The baths are open for men in the morning and for women in the afternoon. This is

a great chance to immerse yourself, quite literally, in ancient history and the entry charge is very reasonable.

FESTIVALS

Every summer, **Le Kef** holds a festival in its great *kasbah* to honour and celebrate the life of its local saint, **Sidi Bou Makhlouf**. At **Sbeitla** (Roman Sufetula) during the last week of July the **Festival of the Seven Abdullahs** is held to mark the victory of Arab Muslim armies over the Orthodox Christian forces of Prefect Gregory at Sufetula in AD 647, an event which marked the triumph of Islam in the Maghreb. Finally, at **Dougga** a major **Festival of Classical Theatre** is held every July/August – details can be obtained from the ONTT (Office National du Tourisme Tunisien) who maintain a website at: www.tourismtunisia.com or from the official Tunisian tourist office (▲ 35).

The South

Getting Your Bearings

The harsh, almost rainless lands of southern Tunisia, though not so far from the Mediterranean, are quite different in every way. The Sahara beckons to the south. There are oasis towns which provide respite from the desert sun and huge *chotts* or salt lakes which make for a fascinating drive. On the coast the famous resort of Île de Jerba offers beaches, hotels and relaxation.

The chief inland city, Gafsa, is the first of a series of vast palm oases as you travel south. These oases have for centuries catered for the camel-driven caravans of traders, but nowadays visitors can enjoy the sanctuary of cool springs and tropical palmeries in comfort. They are situated around the immense and spectacular *chotts*. The causeways that cross these stunningly colourful plains link the oasis towns and give visitors a rare opportunity to experience this diverse scenery.

The southeastern part of Tunisia also has its sharp contrasts. You can enjoy white sandy beaches and luxury hotels on the olive-rich island of Jerba and in the tourist centre of Zarzis. Then there is the austere desert hill region around Medenine and Foum Tataouine where small guest houses are built into what at first appear to be giant sandcastles, the *ksour*, or ancient granaries of the Berbers.

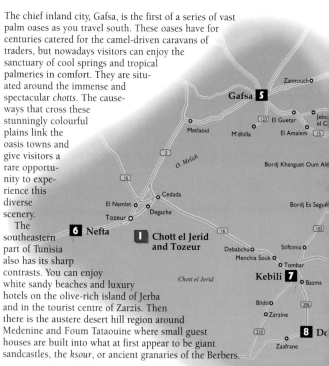

Previous page:
The best
preserved *ksar*
is found at Ksar
Ouled Soltane
Right: The
entrance to the
15th-century
Borj el Kebir in
Houmt Souq

★ Don't Miss

At Your Leisure

A sheep
farmer near
Ghomrassen

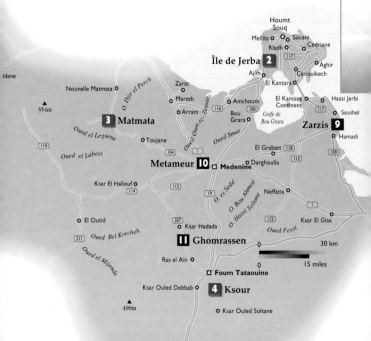

This drive covers some 600km and is best undertaken in a 4WD vehicle. The three-day trip will steer you into the vast salt lakes, stopping at tropical oasis towns, Berber granary castles and then finally on to the coast of the Mediterranean.

The South in Three Days

Day One

Morning
Begin at the oasis town of **⑤ Gafsa** (➤ 146) by visiting the Piscines Romaines (Roman Baths), then drive west via Metlaoui and Moulares, an arid area where a famous railway line passes through the Gorges de Selja (➤ 164). Continue on Route 201 until you reach **Tamerza** (below, ➤ 146). You can stop for a refreshment at the Tamerza Palace hotel (➤ 152) and view the ruins of Tamerza and its oasis from the hotel terrace.

Afternoon
There are two other mountain oases worth visiting: **Midès** (➤ 146) and Chebika. Then take Route 16 and head 60km south over the first of the salt lakes, Chott el Gharsa, to the town of **⑥ Tozeur** (➤ 137). The Palmeraie in Tozeur is an oasis of palm trees and natural wells, the ideal place to stroll or enjoy a picnic.

It's best to set off on the last leg of today's journey an hour before sunset. Drive southeast on Route 16 on the causeway which crosses **⑥ Chott el Jerid** (➤ 136) to **⑦ Kebili** (➤ 147). The changing colours of the salt crystals across the *chott* in the sunset are quite breathtaking.

Evening
After the long journey you may want to relax and enjoy the fine views over the *chott* from the Fort des Autruches hotel's modest restaurant (➤ 150).

Day Two

Morning

Check your tyres, water, oil and petrol as you are going to drive through the desert, heading east out of Kebili on Route 104. The road is usually in reasonable condition, and should be easily navigable if you are driving

a 4WD vehicle. It's a 100km drive to **8 Matmata** (left ➤ 142) where you can have coffee and a snack in the Skywalker Bar of the famous *Star Wars* troglodyte dwelling.

Afternoon

Continue east on Route 104 to **10 Metameur** (➤ 148). This is a good introduction to the **4 *ksour*** (➤ 144), the spectacular fortified granaries designed so that the local Berber farmers could guard their grain stores from attack. It's only a few kilometres into Medenine from where you should plan or book your *ksar* accommodation for the night.

Evening

Experience a night staying in a *ksar*. The best of these rustic guest houses are available in **Ksar el Hallouf** (➤ 145) or **Ksar Hadada** (➤ 145), both slightly more than 30km from Medenine.

Day Three

Morning

From your *ksar* head to Foum Tataouine to see the busy market. From here take Autoroute 19 north to Medenine, then east on Route 118 towards the coast.

Afternoon

When you arrive in **9 Zarzis** (➤ 148), head straight for the beach where you can find a pleasant restaurant or café.

After lunch drive north on Route 117 over the El Kantara Causeway to **2 Île de Jerba** (➤ 139) then continue up the coastal road until you reach the main town, Houmt Souq (right, ➤ 140).

Evening

After covering some 600km by car in three days reward yourself with a glorious meal at one of the island's fine restaurants (➤ 152).

Chott el Jerid and Tozeur

It's difficult to imagine a more breathtaking scene than the drive across the salt lake of the Chott el Jerid. This vast, arid plain constantly changes colour in the sunlight and the resulting mirages will dazzle you. In the midst of this visual feast the only sound you will hear is the echo of silence.

Despite the remoteness of the region, at the end of the day you have the pleasure of stopping at Tozeur, an oasis town in the centre of the salt lakes. But Tozeur is so much more than an oasis. It's a lush town with an ancient history, spectacular views, good museums and an intriguing *médina*.

Chott el Jerid

Tunisia boasts three substantial *chotts* or salt lakes: Chott el Jerid; its eastern branch, Chott el Fejaj; and Chott el Gharsa

to the west. They lie below sea level, surrounded by the desert and by low mountain ranges. It is a desolate, hot region, but strangely attractive.

Chott el Jerid covers roughly 5,000sq km, a vast flat expanse of glistening crystals crossed by a 90km causeway. You can often see shimmering mirages here as you drive along this arrow-straight track. At intervals you will observe rich variations of colour in the crystals depending on weather, time of year and mineral deposits. There might be a clear blue on one side of the road and an amethyst pink on the other. As

Driving across the Chott el Jerid, the largest of the salt lakes

you drive by, the salt crystals gleam and wink in the sun like diamonds. After the rains, the lakes enlarge and become inland salt seas for a while.

Tozeur

Tozeur is the most significant of a string of oases which nestle amid the arid salt lakes. The site is known to have been occupied even in the Stone Age some 10,000 years ago, and for many centuries provided respite for caravans of camels and traders as they crossed the Sahara. In recent years Tozeur has become familiar as the set for a part of the 1996 film *The English Patient*.

The town is built around a large oasis which covers some 1,000ha. As there is now an airport connecting it to both Tunis and Île de Jerba (➤ 139), Tozeur is emerging as a favourite destination for "desert tourism". In fact, there has recently been a fever of hotel development and a *zone touristique* has grown up beside the oasis overlooking the **Palmeraie** (Palmery). Nonetheless, the Palmeraie is a picturesque spot for walking or enjoying a picnic and is said to include 200 spring wells and 266,000 palm trees.

There are views from a large rocky outcrop about 3km southwest of the centre called the **Belvédère**. The 30-minute walk to this viewpoint is rewarded with vistas over both of the neighbouring salt lakes and the Tozeur oasis.

The oasis at Tozeur is the largest and most important in the region

Inside town you'll find the *médina* of Tozeur which is known as Ouled el-Hadef after the local tribe that founded it. Ouled el-Hadef offers the usual intricate network of narrow, winding streets, many of which are dead ends. The 14th-century architecture of this quarter is renowned throughout Tunisia, distinguished by small, yellow, baked bricks made from the local clay which are lavishly decorated in patterns that reflect the local Berber textile designs.

If you only have time to visit one museum while you are in Tozeur go to the **Musée Dar Cheraït**. It is situated on the *Route Touristique* and displays local costumes, jewellery, furniture and other paraphernalia. The museum has created various themed rooms depicting scenes from daily Tunisian life. There is even a sound and light show called "*A Thousand and One Nights*".

TAKING A BREAK

For a light lunch and perhaps some Tozeur specialities try **Les Andalous** (➤ 152), at the Hôtel du Jardin slightly out of town on the road to Kebili.

The minaret of Tozeur's Mosque el Farkous

Tozeur
✚ 182 A3
⊠ 450km south of Tunis
✈ Regular daily flights from Tunis

Palmeraie and Paradis
⊠ 2km south of avenue Abdulkacem Chebbi
🕓 Open access

Belvédère
⊠ 3km southwest of city
🕓 Open access

Musée Dar Cheraït
⊠ Route Touristique
☎ 76 452100
🕓 Daily 8 am–midnight
🎫 Moderate

CHOTT EL JERID AND TOZEUR: INSIDE INFO

Top tips It is strongly recommended that you **rent a 4WD vehicle** to cross this area. Although the causeway (Autoroute 16) is paved, many of the surrounding roads are simply dirt tracks.
• Be sure to fill up with **water and petrol** before setting off.
• A **romantic way** of visiting the oasis and the Palmeraie is by *calèche*, a horse-drawn carriage. Or, one step further, floating overhead in a hot-air balloon (➤ 154).

One to miss Despite its name, the Zoo du Paradis in Tozeur is **quite depressing**, although it is beautifully set alongside the Palmeraie. Even less appealing is the other zoo in town, Zoo Tijani.

2 Île de Jerba

Île de Jerba is an exquisite and idyllic island, connected to the mainland by a 7km-long causeway. The island is said to be the "Land of the Lotus Eaters"; the Greek hero Odysseus was cast ashore and soon discovered that he didn't want to leave. Nowadays Île de Jerba is still proving itself to be irresistible, both to Tunisian and foreign visitors. Equipped with an international airport, this holiday island offers plenty of hotels, sandy beaches and a year-round, pleasant warm climate.

Île de Jerba (Island of Jerba) was always popular: by Carthaginian and Roman times there were settlements here, and in AD 655, with the rest of North Africa, it was conquered by the Arabs. After that it passed to whoever controlled Tunisia, with conquests or invasions by the Normans from Sicily and later by the Spaniards. By the 15th century it had become a pirate fortress, and in the early 16th century was included in Barbarossa's pirate "empire" (► 14).

Jerba is flat, with a climate suitable for growing dates, olives and vines. The sea provides fish, sponges and oysters, and woollen goods such as blankets are also manufactured here.

The west side of the island is rocky and devoid of development, but the east coast is lined with gorgeous beaches, and these continue beyond the causeway southeast to Zarzis (► 148) and the Libyan border. These beaches, and Mellita airport, have made Jerba a very popular destination, and hotels now throng the coasts. Houmt Souq on the north coast is the principal town and market centre. Ajim in the south is the main port.

Silhouetted against the glittering waters, a fisherman casts his net

The island is famous for its 354 mosques (one for each day of the Muslim year) and the ancient synagogue at **La Ghriba** which is said to be 2,500 years old. The mosques are extraordinarily varied in their architecture, but the chief characteristics are the white outer walls, often almost completely blank except for a blue door. They also differ in styles of minaret, and many offer spectacular settings for photography within this island paradise.

If you are not arriving directly at the airport you can reach Île de Jerba either by the ferry to **Ajim**, or a longer route, across the **El Kantara Causeway**. Originally a Carthaginian feat of engineering, this 7km causeway was destroyed by the Turkish pirate Dragut in 1551, and was only repaired in 1953. Ajim is a working fishing and sponge-diving port, as well as the ferry port for the island.

Above: Terracotta pots are used by local fishermen to catch octopus

Houmt Souq

Houmt Souq lies 6km east of the international airport at Mellita. Parts of the town have a French colonial flavour, but the town centre is thoroughly Arabic: a compact nest of attractive, small, whitewashed squares and delightful shopping streets that constitute the local *souq* (market).

The principal attraction is the **Borj el Kebir** (Great Tower), which is an impressive fort overlooking the harbour. In the 13th century the Sicilian Roger de Lauria built a fort here,

Below: Schoolgirls walking near La Ghriba, the old Jewish synagogue

which was improved upon by later occupants. In 1560 the pirate Dragut massacred the Christian defenders at this spot. The fort is an impressive if austere structure, virtually windowless, with imposing towers along the stone walls.

Like many Tunisian towns there is a **Musée des Arts et Traditions Populaires** (Museum of Arts and Popular Traditions). The displays are dedicated to the unique culture of the Jerban people and there is also an interesting pottery workshop. Near by on place d'Algérie sits the Jami' et-Turuk (Mosque of the Turks); non-Muslims are not allowed to enter but can appreciate the strikingly beautiful Ottoman minaret from outside.

An elderly Orthodox Jew relaxes in the Ghriba synagogue

TAKING A BREAK

In Houmt Souq there are several restaurants on place Hédi Chaker offering great seafood, but **The Blue Moon** (➤ 152) is probably the pick of the bunch and you can eat in the open. It also has a wine list with some of the best Tunisian wines available.

✚ 183 E3
✉ 506km south of Tunis ✈ Up to seven flights a day from Tunis

La Ghriba
✉ 8km from Houmt Souq
🕐 Open access Sun–Fri
✋ Free

Musée des Arts et Traditions Populaires
✉ avenue Abdelhamid el Kadhi
☎ 75 650540 🕐 Sat–Thu 8–12, 3–7 (9:30–4:30 in winter)
✋ Moderate

Borj el Kebir
✉ rue Taieb Mehiri, near the harbour
🕐 Sat–Thu 8–12, 3–7 (9:30–4:30 in winter)
✋ Inexpensive

El Kantara Causeway
✉ 30km southwest of Houmt Souq
🕐 Open access
✋ Free

ÎLE DE JERBA: INSIDE INFO

Top tip For those not staying at the *zone touristique* (tourist zone) and who wish to spend a day on a white sandy beach, there is a **lovely public beach** about 10km southeast of Houmt Souq.

3 Matmata

Matmata, an olive-growing centre 43km southwest of Gabès, achieved international fame after it was used as the location for the cave-dwellings in the film *Star Wars*. The houses at Matmata are troglodyte apartments, some of which were cut into the eroded hills perhaps as early as the 4th century BC. Many are still occupied by local Berber families. Their underground situation, like the grand villas of Bulla Regia (► 76), ensures coolness in the summer and warmth in the winter.

Neat stonework marks the entrance to a troglodyte house

Cave-dwelling, or troglodyte people, have occupied lands around North Africa for centuries. Originally, they took to building homes in the ground because it was easier to burrow into the crumbling rock than to cut blocks from it. More significantly, the caves offered protection from the searing heat; most dwellings can maintain a temperature of 17°C all year round. The houses are cut at different levels into the rock and are usually decorated simply with the occasional arch or with white trimmings to windows or doorways, and perhaps a blue "Hand of Fatima" to bring luck.

There are tours to Matmata daily and the locals are accustomed to dealing with strangers in their living rooms. If you are not on an organised tour you will have to make a private arrangement with the owner of a troglodyte house or at least buy some of his or her handicrafts. Alternatively, you can experience troglodyte living by staying at one of the hotels that have been constructed by amalgamating dwellings into multi-court complexes: The **Marhala** is part of the Touring Club de Tunisie chain; the **Sidi Driss** (► 150) achieved fame for its outlandish Skywalker Bar; and there is a third hotel called **Les Berbères**. Staying overnight in a troglodyte hotel is an experience you will never forget.

Around Matmata

If you take a trip southwards from Matmata on some of the smaller roads, there are several charming villages among the hills. One such town, **Toujane**, on the road to Medenine, has many ruined houses, but there are a few shops selling bright, multicoloured carpets.

Tamezret, west of Matmata, is a small hilltop village clustered around the tomb of a local saint named Sidi Haj Yusuf.

This is a very scenic region, bordering the area where the troglodyte dwellings begin.

TAKING A BREAK

It just has to be the **Sidi Driss** (► 150), once voted "One of the World's Weirdest Hotels". The bar was the setting for the famous "Alien Jazz Club" scene in the movie *Star Wars*. Take a troglodyte seat and select one of the Star Wars cocktails.

A woman grinds grain inside one of the restored troglodyte dwellings

➕ 183 D2
✉ 45km southwest of Gabès on Route 107
🚌 Up to ten buses a day from Gabès

MATMATA: INSIDE INFO

Top tip Not all locals living in Matmata benefit from tourism, nor do they appreciate being photographed and invaded every day. It is advisable to be understanding and **remember that these are their homes**. You may even have to exercise patience as it appears that some Matmata locals – especially children – have been reduced to abusing and swearing at visitors.

4 Ksour

Monts des Ksour is a French-Arabic name meaning "Mountains of the Castles". The mountains lie scattered around the town of Foum Tataouine and among these hills are the so-called castles or *ksour*. These *ksour* are actually the Berbers' old fortified grain stores which were built not only to preserve grain but to defend the supplies from rival tribes. It is said that some of the oldest *ksour* (singular *ksar*) may be up to 800 years old.

The climate in this region is often unbearably hot and a good harvest might have to be preserved meticulously to compensate for bad years. Local Berbers therefore zealously guarded their grain in these stone and mud edifices. The barrel-vaulted chambers, sometimes on three or four levels connected by stairways, were ideal for the preservation of the grain. The chambers (*ghurfa*, Arabic for "room") faced on to one or more courtyards, usually with a fortified gatehouse. The *ghurfa* later became dwelling houses, but many were abandoned as security came to the country and the effort of living high on a *ksar* became unnecessary.

The converted *ghurfa* of the Hotel Ksar Hadada

Ksar Ouled Soltane

The best preserved and most picturesque granary is Ksar Ouled Soltane, south of Tatouine, perched on a hill above a rocky valley. When you enter you will find two courtyards, one attributed to the 16th century, and the other the mid-19th century. The façade is amazing; a series of rooms with the *ghurfa* piled one above the other to the height of three or four storeys.

Other Ksour

If you want to embark on a tour of these ancient granaries then you will need a 4WD vehicle as several are located in desert areas with poor roads. The best place to base yourself is in Medenine or Foum Tataouine. There are at least a dozen sites dotted around the arid countryside.

Ksar el Hallouf is said to have originated in the 13th century. It lies to the west near Jebel Mogor. A part of the old granary has been converted into a very basic but friendly guest house.

Ksar Hadada shares the distinction with Matmata (► 142) of being a location in a *Star Wars* movie. Since then this charming labyrinth of alleyways and courtyards has fallen into disrepair, although at least one aficionado has tried to open it up again as a guest house.

A carpenter at work outside one of the few remaining *ksar*

TAKING A BREAK

Facilities at the *ksour* are often rudimentary at best, so you may wish to treat yourself to a meal in Medenine or Foum Tataouine on your way to or from the sites. Medenine's best food can be found at Hôtel Ibis. In Foum Tataouine you will find the Sangho hotel (► 151) very reliable. It also has a swimming pool.

Ksar Ouled Soltane
➕ 183 E1
✉ 20km southeast of Tataouine
Ⓐ Open access

☎ 75 647037
Ⓐ Open access

Ksar Hadada
➕ 183 D2
✉ 25km northeast of Foum Tataouine on Route 207
Ⓐ Open access

Ksar el Hallouf
➕ 183 D2 ✉ 40km west of Medenine on Route 114

KSOUR: INSIDE INFO

Top tip At the time of writing there were **no car rental agencies** in either Medenine or Foum Tataouine. The nearest centre where cars are available for rent is on Île de Jerba (► 139).

At Your Leisure

⑤ Gafsa

Gafsa, the largest Tunisian oasis and a regional centre with a population of 80,000, encloses a substantial grove of date palms and other irrigated fruit trees. Cereals, esparto grass and olives are also cultivated around here.

The town was the centre for the mesolithic stone industry, first found at nearby El-Mekta, and dated around 6250 BC. It became a Berber town of considerable strength and reputation but was destroyed by the Romans in 106 BC and replaced by the Roman colony of Capsa. Nowadays visitors generally pass through it on their way to the oases, the salt lakes and the desert.

The 15th-century *kasbah* (fortress) is a substantial walled structure. Near by you'll find the **Piscines Romaines** (Roman Baths). The baths are quite remarkable, comprising two large sunken pools and a *hammam*. In a pleasant square beside the baths there is a modest museum mainly

The ruins of the abandoned town of Tamerza

devoted to the flint industry and local Roman artefacts.

Leaving Gafsa and heading west towards the Algerian border there are two quaint mountain oasis villages. **Midès**, the northernmost, overlooks an impressive gorge. Berber one-room dwellings, most of them abandoned, hang giddily over it. The palm oasis is a delightful haven of shade filled with date palms, orange trees, pomegranates and figs. Some houses are being restored as tourist accommodation or shops for local handicrafts.

Close by to the southeast is the oasis town of **Tamerza** which has a waterfall, a pristine white mosque and the tomb of a *marabout* (holy man). Tamerza is now almost completely abandoned since flooding devastated the town in 1969, and the quiet streets have an eerie air about them.

⊞ 182 B3 93km northeast of Tozeur

Piscines Romaines
✉ avenue Habib Bourguiba
🕐 Tue–Sun 8–12, 3 –7 (9:30 –4:30 in winter) 🎟 Inexpensive

Midès
⊞ 182 A3 ✉ 75km west of Gafsa on Route 201 🕐 Open access

Tamerza
⊞ 182 A3 ✉ 75km west of Gafsa, 5km southeast of Midès 🕐 Open access
🎟 Free

6 Nefta

Nefta has two oases. One, Qasr el Aïn, is a giant palm-filled crater, linked with an even larger oasis comprising a 10sq km garden of palm trees. Situated on the edge of the salt lake Chott El Jerid (► 136), they contain 230,000 palm trees and are watered by 152 wells and springs, some hot and sulphurous. There is even a bathing pool, with cafés overlooking it, and winding paths among the palm trees and fertile agricultural gardens where you can stroll at sunset. Unfortunately the wells are running dry and many locals blame tourism and swimming pools.

Nefta is also an important religious centre for Sufi devotees. It is a town of mosques, dotted with the white-domed shrines of *marabouts* (holy men). The Zaouia de Sidi Brahim (Shrine of Sidi Brahim) is the local centre for one of the Sufi orders. There is also a mosque, Mosquée de Sidi M'Khareg which is situated overlooking the palms.
⊞ 182 A3 ✉ 25km west of Tozeur on Autoroute 3 🕐 Open access 🎟 Free

7 Kebili

Another beautiful Berber oasis, Kebili was once an important slave market, then a French garrison town that became one of President Habib Bourguiba's (► 18) places of exile.

Kebili's lush palmery is irrigated from a spring which lies north of the town. Just outside the town centre on the road to Douz is a Roman bathing pool and a *hammam* (Turkish bath) which receives its water from a deep bore hole.
⊞ 182 C2 ✉ 100km east of Tozeur, 100km south of Gafsa, 100km east of Gabès 🕐 Open access 🎟 Free

8 Douz

Douz lies at the edge of the 'real' desert of sand dunes, and is the southernmost of the main oases. A few kilometres south of town you can visit the so-called Great Dune, where it's possible to rent a quad bike or take a short camel ride. Nowadays a good road gives access to Matmata across almost 100km of desert route, emerging into hills with the occasional palm tree.

The town of Douz has traditionally survived on date production, although the arrival of tourism has encouraged several new businesses and nowadays shops line the main street selling attractive carpets and blankets. The **Musée de Douz** (Museum of Douz) offers some idea of desert life with a display of camel equipment and a Bedouin tent, as well as local costumes and jewellery.
⊞ 182 C2 ✉ 35km south of Kebili 🕐 Open access 🎟 Free

Musée de Douz
✉ avenue des Martyrs 🕐 Mon–Sat 8:30–1, 3–6 🎟 Inexpensive

A fine selection of grains and pulses at a market in Douz

❾ Zarzis

This beach resort lies on the peninsula south of Île de Jerba. There are long stretches of sandy beach and a *zone touristique* has been created, complete with large glittering hotel complexes.

Zarzis' pristine beach attracts all ages

Zarzis was developed as a French garrison town, successor to a Turkish fortress whose foundations now support the Grande Mosquée (Great Mosque). The town itself is rather dull but it does have the added advantage of being a tax-free zone which makes it popular for shopping.

➕ 183 F2 ✉ 50km south of Houmt Souq on Route 109 ⓒ Open access 🎟 Free

❿ Metameur

The *ksar* (granary castle) here is said to be 600 years old, and survives in good shape. It is the first of the really impressive castles as you travel southwards. The piled-up, vaulted stone chambers rise to three stories around all four sides of a rather desolate square. A section of this *ksar* has been converted into a hotel, whose Berber owners also arrange trips to some of the outlying granary castles, or *ksour* (➤ 144). Behind the *ksar* is a pretty barrel-vaulted mosque.

➕ 183 E2 ✉ 8km northwest of Medenine on Route 104 ⓒ Open access 🎟 Free

⓫ Ghomrassen

The outcrop of Ghomrassen shelters some of the local Berbers' *ksour* (➤ 144). Ghomrassen is a small commercial town expanding rapidly with new houses, some with cave dwellings behind. At the base of the outcrop you can see a series of vaulted structures, some eviscerated by time, others still occupied. Above them, in a perilous state of decomposition, the cliff rises. Right at the top, painted white and with a little domed turret, the *qubba* (tomb) of the *marabout* (holy man) Sidi Moussa ibn Abdallah helps to protect the people below.

➕ 183 E1 ✉ 25km northwest of Foum Tataouine on Route 221 ⓒ Open access 🎟 Free

A whitewashed tomb near Ghomrassen

Where to... Stay

Prices

Expect to pay for a standard double room per night
£ under TD50   ££ TD50–TD100   £££ over TD100

The South has a fine selection of hotels and is well known for its *marhalas* (inexpensive traditional hotels). These use old buildings such as the fortified granaries in Metameur, or the troglodyte dwellings in Matmata. Houmt Souq on Jerba Island has an array of really delightful hotels, including some splendid *caravanserais* converted into modern hotels.

DOUZ

Oasis el-Mouradi £££

Perhaps the best hotel in town, or rather some small distance out of town as it's set in the middle of the *zone touristique*. Rooms are modern and well-appointed, with air-conditioning, private bathrooms, cable television and mini-bars. There's a decent swimming pool, a couple of bars, and a reasonable international and Tunisian restaurant.

✚ **182 C2** ◻ **Zone Touristique**
☎ **75 470303; fax: 75 470905; email: meharidouz@planet.tn**

Saharien ££

An isolated hotel with small, tidy bungalows set in the middle of the extensive palmery to the southwest of town. The newer southern wing is the most modern and comfortable part of the hotel, so request a room here. Facilities include a swimming pool, but the main attraction is being in the heart of Douz' very extensive palm groves – there are said to be more than 400,000 of them, so this is a real oasis setting.

✚ **182 C2** ◻ **rue de la Palmeraie**
☎ **75 471337; fax: 75 470339**

Touareg ££

Located in the up-market *zone touristique* to the south of Douz, the Touareg has plenty of character as it's built in the style of a medieval *kasbah*, complete with crenellated walls and small turrets. The rooms are among the most luxurious in town, and the swimming pool has an artificial island with palm trees in the middle of it.

✚ **182 C2** ◻ **Zone Touristique**
☎ **75 470057; fax: 75 470313**

GAFSA

Gafsa ££

The Gafsa is a middle-rank hotel providing perfectly clean and adequate accommodation but without much character. Room rates include breakfast, and the downtown location is convenient for easy access to avenue Taieb Mehiri, the pedestrian area and market. All rooms are air-conditioned and some have satellite television.

✚ **182 B3** ◻ **rue Ahmed Snoussi**
☎ **76 224000; fax: 76 224747**

La Lune £

This is one of Gafsa's less expensive hotels attracting mainly budget travellers. Breakfast is included in the rate, but the bar is also the main nightspot in town. Alcoholic drinks served tend to be local rather than imported, but if you want a drink away from the *zone touristique*, this is about as good as it gets.

✚ **182 B3** ◻ **rue Jamel Abdennaceur**
☎ **76 220218; fax: 76 220980**

Maamoun £££

The Maamoun is the best hotel in town, with modern, clean, but

KEBILI

Fort des Autruches ££

A popular place to stay, this battlemented ex-fort on the southeastern side of town retains pleasing suggestions of the *Beau Geste* or French Foreign Legion era. There's a swimming pool and terrace, as well as a bar overlooking the oasis and the more distant salt lakes. The management can organise desert rides and trips.

✛ 182 C2 ☒ route de Douz ☎ 75 491117; fax: 75 491295

MATMATA

Sidi Driss ££

The Sidi Driss at Matmata is the hotel whose bar achieved fame as the outlandish alien jazz club in the film *Star Wars*. The bar is now known as the Skywalker Bar. A typical underground troglodyte dwelling of the region, it has halls, passages, staircases, courts and rooms, including the bar, dug into

the rock. It is perhaps more interesting than attractive, with a slightly claustrophobic air, but even if you don't want to stay there, a visit and a drink in the bar is well worthwhile.

✛ 183 D2 ☒ Centre of Matmata, ☎ 75 230005; fax: 75 230265

TAMERZA

Les Cascades £

This is a unique and unusual hotel, with its curious palm-thatched accommodation lying above a little waterfall and stream within the village. It's a very beautiful location. Rooms are simple but clean, and the reliable Restaurant Chedli nearby provides good Tunisian and Franco-Tunisian fare. Other facilities include a pool.

✛ 182 A3 ☒ rue de les Cascades ☎ 76 485322

Tamerza Palace £££

Nothing in this area can compare in luxury with the Tamerza Palace,

with its bizarre, pinnacled exterior architecture, its cool, pleasant and agreeably laid-out interior and its terrace with swimming pool looking directly over the *wadi* on to the ruined village opposite. It is a largish hotel for the area, and surprisingly good for this remote place.

✛ 182 A3 ☒ Just outside Tamerza, ☎ 76 453722; fax: 76 435845, www.tamerza-palace.com

TOZEUR

Grand Hotel de l'Oasis ££

There's no shortage of first-class hotels in Tozeur with plenty of top-rank places out along avenue 7 Novembre, but the Grand Hotel is more centrally located for the old town and has plenty of character. Its traditional brickwork is discreetly illuminated at night to good effect. Food in the restaurant is fine and the service friendly.

✛ 182 A3 ☒ 1 avenue Abdulkacem Chebbi and avenue Habib Bourguiba ☎ 76 452300; fax: 76 452153

rather characterless air-conditioned rooms. Facilities include an attractive swimming pool and small business centre. There is a choice of bars and restaurants, and the management are both knowledgeable and helpful in arranging tours and excursions.

✛ 182 B3 ☒ avenue Taieb Mehiri ☎ 76 224441; fax: 76 226440

ÎLE DE JERBA

Erriadh ££

Particularly recommended for those who might like something with an Arab flavour, and the suggestion of a vanished past, this converted *funduq* is perfect. All rooms are air-conditioned and beautifully decorated. Tiling abounds, adding rich colours to the rooms and the exterior. Because of the Erriadh's popularity it's best to book in advance.

✛ 183 E3 ☒ rue Mohamed el-Ferjani, Houmt Souq ☎ 75 650756; fax: 75 650487

Where to...
Eat and Drink

Prices

Expect to pay per person for a standard three-course meal, excluding drinks and service charges

£ under TD15   ££ TD15–TD30   £££ over TD30

DOUZ

La Rosa £

Enduringly popular with visitors, this restaurant serves simple food, both Tunisian and international, at very reasonable prices. During the summer months a Bedouin tent is set up to provide shade and atmosphere. In the colder winter months you're better off indoors. La Rosa is a good place for a simple breakfast of French bread and fried eggs or for a hearty dinner.

✚ 182 C2 ⊠ avenue du 7 Novembre
☎ 75 495465 ⏰ 8:30–1:30, 5–10

Rendezvous £

Apart from the hotel restaurants, the Rendezvous, situated on the main street, is probably the most elegant establishment in Douz, although it is still quite a plain sort of place with some roadside tables outside. It serves the usual grilled meats, kebabs and other Tunisian favourites.

✚ 182 C2 ⊠ avenue Taieb Mehiri
⏰ Daily 7 am–7.30 pm

Restaurant Ali Baba £

An attractive local café with outdoor seating set in a shaded courtyard. The usual selection of local dishes is offered including spicy *merguez* sausage, *couscous*, omelettes and slices of pizza. No alcohol is served, so try the hot mint tea instead.

✚ 182 C2 ⊠ rue Kebili ⏰ Daily 7 am–7.30 pm; closed during Ramadan

FOUM TATAOUINE

Sangho ££

This stylish restaurant, decorated with antiques, pseudo-antiques and bits of Tunisian desert bric-à-brac, is attached to the Sangho hotel. They are used to dealing with visiting tour groups as well as private travellers, and offer a good selection of Franco-Tunisian-Italian cuisine, as well as a chance for a cold beer in this out-of-the-way spot. One local speciality you might care to try is the camel meat *couscous* which is surprisingly tender

✚ 183 E1 ⊠ rue Chenini km 3 ☎ 75 860124; fax: 75 862177 ⏰ 11.30–2, 5.30–10.30

GAFSA

Khafallah £

This restaurant in the Khafallah hotel is very popular locally, and therefore can be rather full and noisy, albeit friendly. Simple Tunisian fare, including couscous and kebabs, served at very reasonable prices. Good, refreshing mint tea is always available.

✚ 182 B3 ⊠ rue Mohamed Khadouna. ☎ 76 221468 ⏰ 10–2, 4.30–10.30

Semiramis £

There are several restaurants opposite the *souq* and behind the Gafsa hotel, including the Semiramis. This has long been recommended by local people as one of the best places in town. Service is good and friendly, and the food comprises simple Tunisian and French dishes, as well as pizza and macaroni.

✚ 182 B3 ⊠ rue Ahmed Snoussi ☎ 76 221009 ⏰ 10:30–2:30, 5–11:30

ÎLE DE JERBA

Blue Moon ££

The Blue Moon is a pleasant restaurant in Houmt Souq where you can dine in the open. Local seafood specialities on the menu include lobster, prawns, octopus, crayfish and crab, as well as a good selection of imported and Tunisian wines. It fits into the middle range as far as price goes, although it's always easy to spend more by indulging in good wines, of which this restaurant holds a number.

➕ 183 E3 ☒ place Hedi Chaker, Houmt Souq ☎ 75 650559 ⊚ Daily 11–2:30, 6–11

Hasdrubal ££

A very smart hotel with an elegant and sophisticated restaurant serving authentic French *haute cuisine*

as well as Italian dishes, international favourites and local Tunisian dishes. Seafood of various sorts is the house speciality. This establishment has a good wine list which includes imported as well as local wines, ice-cold beer and a selection of spirits and cocktails. Not cheap, but a good place to celebrate.

➕ 183 E3 ☒ Hasdrubal Hotel, plage Sidi Mahres ☎ 75 657650; fax: 75 657730 ⊚ Daily 11–2:30, 6–11:30

Patisserie M'hirsi La Viennoise ££

How much you might spend here depends as much on the sweetness of your tooth as on how long you have been without authentic French-style pastries and cakes. This attractive *patisserie* has a great range of delights from chocolate to cheesecake, éclairs to fresh fruit tarts. French bread and croissants are also on sale.

➕ 183 E3 ☒ avenue Abdelhamid al-Kadhi, Houmt Souq ⊚ Mon–Sat 9–2, 5–8:30

Restaurant du Sud ££

A friendly, well-appointed locale with spaghetti, pizza, Tunisian-style macaroni, seafood including fish *couscous*, steak and chips, fried chicken and a good selection of salads. Cold beer is generally available and sometimes there may be an imported wine on offer, though usually it will be a local vintage.

➕ 183 E3 ☒ Off place Hedi Chaker, Houmt Souq ☎ 75 650479 ⊚ Daily 11–2:30, 5:30–11

Restaurant La Mamma £

Very popular with locals and independent travellers alike, this friendly restaurant specialises in no-frills local dishes such as *lablabi* or chickpea soup and Tunisian-style macaroni. Fried chicken, fish *couscous* and freshly made-to-order sandwiches stuffed with cheese and garlic sausage (made from beef, not pork) are all reasonably priced and delicious.

➕ 183 E3 ☒ rue Habib Bougatfa ⊚ 11–2, 5:30–9:30

TAMERZA

Tamerza Palace ££–£££

At Tamerza hungry visitors can settle down with a drink at the well-stocked bar of the Tamerza Palace hotel. After your drink go on to eat in the restaurant or on the terrace of this very agreeable hotel. Local and international dishes are served, and alcohol is available.

➕ 182 A3 ☒ Just outside Tamerza ☎ 76 453722; fax: 76 435845 ⊚ 11–2:30; 5:30–11

TOZEUR

Les Andalous ££

This excellent establishment, attached to the Hotel du Jardin, is generally considered to be one of the best restaurants in southern Tunisia. Dishes served include French and Italian specialities as well as local Tunisian cooking.

➕ 182 A3 ☒ rue Kebili ☎ 76 454196; fax: 76 454199 ⊚ Daily 11–2:30, 5:30–10:30

Where to...
Shop

SOUQS

In **Houmt Souq**, a town in which the old centre is almost all market, there is a great deal to delight the eye, and many good opportunities to add to your collection of souvenirs. **Carpets** figure prominently, including some beautifully coloured and intricately patterned *kilims*, and there are jewellery stalls selling gold and silver, including silverware "**hands of Fatima**", an Islamic talisman popular throughout Tunisia. Items made from coral are for sale, as well as sea shells and other protected natural products; these are best avoided (▶ 174). There's also a wide range of leather goods and some attractive basket-ware.

The local **ceramics** of Guellala, made in the south of the island, can be bought here too. The best buys include plates, bowls, vases and tiles. The latter, if you buy several, can make a very attractive wall panel back home. There are one or two rather splendid **antique shops**, but the prices many potential customers are put off and don't even bother bargaining.

As usual, if haggling doesn't appeal (and Houmt Souq merchants are an unusually tough bunch to bargain with), then head out to the **SOCOPA** shop (open 8:30–noon, 4–7) on avenue Habib Bourguiba by the junction with rue Jamaa Echeik. In southern Tunisia Houmt Souq is also the best place for items other than souvenirs. **International newspapers** are for sale on avenue Habib Bourguiba about 100m south of SOCOPA. Also in the south of town there's a good fruit and vegetable market in the winding *passage des souqs*. The best

supermarket in town is **Monosouq** on avenue Abdelhamid el-Kadhi, while there's another good outlet for imported foodstuffs and wines at the supermarket on rue Mohammed Badra.

Near **Tamerza** you will find the **Waterfall Market**. To reach it exit the town on the road towards Chebika; you'll soon come to the waterfall. Here there is an extensive collection of stalls selling a variety of attractive things, including brightly coloured ceramics, roses of the desert, glassware, jewellery, small *kilims* and so on.

CARPETS

Several towns in the south make carpets as a local speciality. **Houmt Souq** has several splendid, but usually quite expensive carpet shops in the main tourist souq. **Toujane**, a small village southeast of Matmata, might make a better alternative if you are set on buying a carpet. It has a number of shops exhibiting

beautiful and richly coloured carpets and better prices can generally be obtained in Toujane than in Houmt Souq, especially with a little enthusiastic bargaining. **Gafsa**, too, has a good selection of attractive carpets and woven blankets for sale. Just beyond the famous Piscines Romaines (Roman Baths), in avenue Habib Bourguiba, Mansoor Daab runs a well-known and reputable shop selling a good variety of carpets. **Douz** also has several shops on its main street hung with attractive carpets and blankets, while **Oudref** too has a reputation for *kilims* and local blankets.

The south has a reputation for producing some of the best-quality leatherwork in the country, and the souqs at Houmt Souq and Gafsa are good places to purchase both leather goods and basketry. If you want to taste really delicious dates, the real staple of life throughout the desert world, then buy them in the oasis markets of Douz, Tozeur or Gafsa.

Where to...
Be Entertained

The chief pleasures of the south seem to be strolling through the markets, dining in the local restaurants, or just sitting having coffee in a café. More formal entertainment such as meals served by waiters in Arab costumes with traditional music in the background is offered at the larger tourist hotels and resorts, but beyond this nighttime activities are simple and limited.

NIGHTLIFE

Out along Jerba's *zone touristique* the huge **Dar Jerba** hotel has numerous bars as well as a large disco and even offers Bavarian folk evenings. In the same area the **Hasdrubal** hotel (▶ 152) has a good poolside bar and a disco. At **Gafsa**, the main (indeed just about only) night spot is the bar at **La Lune** hotel (▶ 149). In **Tozeur** the **Chiraz Bar** on avenue Farhat Hached serves cold beer and other alcoholic drinks into the evening, as does the much more up-market **les Andalous** on the Kebili road (▶ 152). If one bar stands out in the south as a "must visit" destination, on Jerba, it's the **Skywalker Bar** in **Matmata**'s Sidi Driss hotel (▶ 150). Here you can enjoy a "Star War" perched on one of the troglodyte seats made famous in the first of the *Star Wars* epics.

tion about sand yachting and expeditions by camel or 4-wheel-drive vehicles into the Sahara. The gorge between **Tamerza** and **Mides** is ideal for a donkey ride or a walk if you avoid the heat and take a good supply of water. The local Tamerza hotels can supply the donkeys and guides. **Nefta** and **Tozeur** offer camel rides of longer or shorter duration and in each place there are organised tours that supply all that is needed, including the indispensable guides.

At **Douz**, the gateway to the Tunisian Sahara, the great appeal is **camel trekking.** Rides can be organised from one hour to overnight in length. The latter involves camping, cooking by an open fire in the desert and sleeping beneath the star-strewn desert sky at night which is something to be experienced! There are several agencies in town that can arrange camel treks; **Voyages Douz** at 3, avenue Taieb Mehiri (tel: 75 495315) can be recommended.

Douz hosts a dramatic and highly photogenic **National Sahara Festival** in late December, with Berbers in full costume supplying musical, camel and horse-riding (and fighting) displays and other events. Also in December **Tozeur** has its **Festival of the Oases.** In March, there is a **Festival des Ksour** at **Tatouine**. Details about all these can be obtained from the local Tourism Offices (▶ 35) or by visiting: www.tourismtunisia.com

At **Midoun**, on Jerba, you can see a **Berber wedding procession.** with the appropriate music and costumes, staged every Tuesday afternoon.

The **Aeroasis Club** (tel: 76 452361) at **Tozeur**, offers hot-air balloon flights. The Tourism Offices and some of the hotels in the different desert towns can also give informa-

Walks & Tours

1 TUNIS MÉDINA

Walk

The *médina* in Tunis guards an older way of life by its very design. Cars and vehicles cannot penetrate the maze of streets and alleyways. Instead, throngs of people walking, shopping and talking animate the scene, and the noises and smells derive from the work of the copper beaters, perfumes and spices. This walk takes you on a dizzy route in and out of the twisting *souqs* and past most of the major sights of Tunis.

DISTANCE 2km **TIME** 3 hours
START/END POINT Bab el Bahr ✚ 178 C3

1–2

Enter the *médina* (Old City) by the eastern gate or Bab el Bahr in the place de la Victoire. You are faced with two streets.
Forking to the left is rue Jemaa ez Zitouna and to the

right is rue de la Kasbah. Take rue Jemaa ez Zitouna and go straight ahead to the Souq el Fekka in front of the **Jemaa ez Zitouna** (Great Mosque) (▶ 60). If you arrive before noon you can go inside and look around this most impressive building.

2–3

Turn right and follow the façade of the mosque, then left to enter the

vaulted Souq el Attarine. A little way along you'll spot the Souq el Blaghjia, the slippermakers' market, which turns off to the right. Continue straight on into the Souq et Trouk, the Turks' market, where weavers and tailors ply their trade. On the right here is the well-known Café M'rabet (▶ 65), with a restaurant upstairs offering lovely views of the *médina*.

The street leads on to the Souq el Berka, the former slave market which now specialises in jewellery, but you should turn right into the Souq

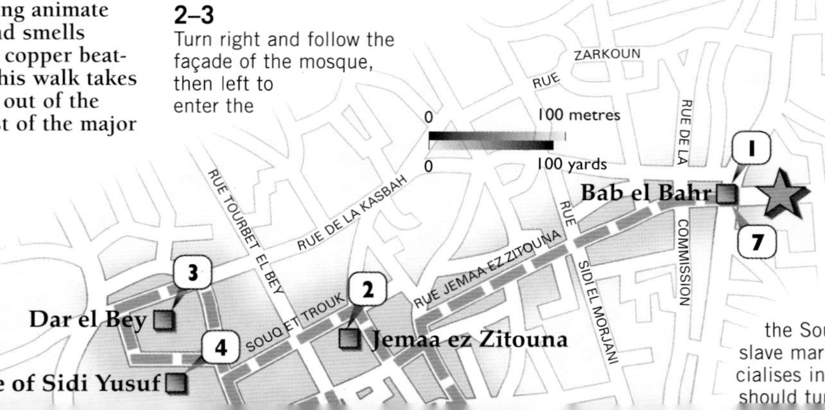

Dar el Bey

Mosque of Sidi Yusuf

Jemaa ez Zitouna

Bab el Bahr

RUE DE LA COMMISSION

RUE DE LA KASBAH

RUE TOURBET EL BEY

SOUQ ET TROUK

RUE JEMAA EZ ZITOUNA

RUE JEMAA EZ ZITOUNA

ZARKOUN

RUE

SIDI EL MORJANI

0   100 metres
0   100 yards

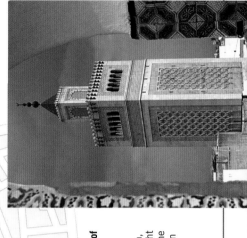

el Bey. On your left side you will see the **Dar el Bey**, the house of the *bey* (the governor during Ottoman rule). Walk past this to the corner of rue de la Kasbah.

3–4

Turn left on rue de la Kasbah and directly in front of you is the place du Gouvernement, a pleasant square with fountains, surrounded by the Prime Minister's Office and other government ministries. You are now standing at the western gate to the *médina*. Take a stroll

Method to the Madness

The maze of market streets is not arranged at random, there is a principle behind their positioning. The "noble trades" take precedence, and are allotted places nearest the sanctuary (in this case, Jemaa ez Zitouna). Directly in front of Jemaa ez Zitouna is the Souq el Fekka which sells dried fruits, and on the northern side of the mosque the *souq* (market) of the perfumeries also enjoys a central role. Lesser trades occupy peripheral streets, and trades that create bad smells, such as tanners, are relegated to the outskirts.

around the square until you are facing south on rue Sidi Ben Ziad. You will pass the hospital, Hôpital Aziza Othmana, on your right. Take a moment to look up at the octagonal minaret of the **Mosque of Sidi Yusuf.**

4–5

Now turn left at the corner of Souq el Leffa, the carpet makers' market. You are now right behind the Great Mosque. Turn right into the Souq des Femmes, and continue straight on

The heavy, square tower of the Jemaa ez Zitouna, built in 1894

Dar Othman

Dar Ben Abdallah

Jemaa el Jedid

Tourbet el Bey

L'BEY

RUE MEHKTAR

RUE DES JUGES

6

5

towards the southern part of the *médina*. The road runs directly into rue Tourbet el Bey, and on your right you will pass the domed Msjid el Koubba, where Ibn Khaldoun, the great Arab historian and resident of Tunis, is said to have prayed. No more than 300m along this road you'll come to one of Tunis's main attractions, the royal tombs of the **Tourbet el Bey**.

5–6

On leaving the Tourbet el Bey turn right out of the door and follow the fine stone walls of the building round to the right. When you have passed the back of the building, turn left into rue Sidi Kacem. Along here you will pass the **Dar Ben Abdallah**, a mansion housing the **Musée des Arts Populaires et Traditions**

A craftsman making a *chechia*, a traditional Tunisian red felt hat

(Museum of Popular Arts and Traditions; ▶ 53). Continue along to the end of rue Sidi Kacem. You will see the Jemaa el Jedid mosque (also known as Mosquée des Teinturiers) on the left, beside the Souq el Bela, the street of cakes and *pâtis-series*. You are now on rue des Teinturiers. Turn left in front of the mosque, then right into a small square where you will find the entrance to the attractive **Dar Othman** (▶ 51), another local mansion that now houses the old city's conservation department.

6–7

Heading north back towards Jemaa ez Zitouna look out for a street on your left called rue de la Medersa es-Slimania. Take this street, then another quick right turn and you'll find your-self looking at the courtyard of **Medersa du Palmier**, one of the three famous *madrassas* or schools of Islamic study. Opposite is a well-known *hammam* or bathhouse, the Hammam Kachachine.

A brightly lit jewellers shop on the busy rue Jemaa ez Zitouna

Walking around the *madrassa* to the right brings you back to the eastern wall of the *médina*. Turn left and follow Souq el Belat back to the Bab el Bahr.

Taking a Break

For a coffee break or lunch try the **Café M'Rabet** (▶ 65), an old Ottoman café in the Souq et Trouq.

2 THE RUINS OF CARTHAGE

Walk

The mighty Phoenician city of Carthage was destroyed by Roman legions in 146 BC. What rose from its ashes during Roman times lies scattered around this suburb of Tunis. An invigorating walk will take you round all the major Roman sights of Carthage and paint a picture in your mind of how magnificent this city once was.

DISTANCE 5km **TIME** 4 hours
START/END POINT Carthage Hannibal Metro Station ✚ 181 D3

1–2

Most visitors to Carthage come in via Tunis. The best place to start is at the Carthage Hannibal Metro Station, which is on the Tunis Marine TGM line direct from Ville Nouvelle (▲ 54) in the centre of Tunis. Coming out of the Metro station you are right in the middle of avenue Habib Bourguiba and you can see the Cathédrale de St-Louis on top of Byrsa Hill in front of you. To get to **Byrsa Hill** (▲ 56) cross the road and turn right. Follow avenue de l'Amphithéâtre for 300m then turn left and wind your way up the hill.

On top of the hill you come to two of Carthage's main sights: firstly the **Musée National de Carthage** (▲ 56) and then the **Cathédrale de St Louis**, now a cultural centre. From here you can look down over the modern town and the sea coast, and understand why the Carthaginians chose this wonderful viewpoint as the centre of their city.

2–3

Looking inland to the west you will see the oval-shaped stadium of the Amphithéâtre des Martyrs about 1km away. Continue on the

Before you Begin…
One Ticket: Seven Sights

If you have time, a visit to all the attractions of Carthage is a worthwhile experience. You can buy one ticket which gives you free entrance to seven of the main sights: the Musée National de Carthage (National Museum of Carthage); the Amphithéâtre des Martyrs (Amphitheatre of the Martyrs); the Théâtre d'Hadrian (Hadrian's Theatre); the Parc Archéologique des Villas Romaines (Archaeological Park of Roman Villas); the Tophet; the Musée Oceanographique (Oceanographic Museum); and the Thermes d'Antonin Pius (Antonine Baths). You can buy the discount ticket at the entrance to any of these sights.

A Roman sculpture of Silenus and Maenad in the Musée National de Carthage

winding road from Byrsa Hill westwards on rue Pasteur. This downhill walk takes you alongside the **Parc Archéologique de Byrsa** back down on to avenue de l'Amphithéâtre. Turn left and follow the perimeter of the archaeological park. Cross the rue de Carthage and continue for 150m to the junction of avenue 7 Novembre. Veer left for another 100m and you will come to the **Amphithéâtre des Martyrs**.

3–4

After a walk around the site, double back on avenue 7 Novembre until you get to rue de Carthage. Turn left and walk 200m to the **Citernes de la Malga** (Malga Cisterns), which used to store the ancient city's water nearly 2,000 years ago. The cisterns were fed via an aqueduct which carried the water from its source in the mountains at Zaghouan 55km away, a fantastic feat of Roman engineering.

Thermes d'Antonin Pius ⑥

Parc Archéologique des Villas Romaines ⑤

Théâtre d'Hadrian

AVENUE HABIB BOURGUIBA

RUE ALI BELHAOUANE

RUE MOHAMMED ALI

AVENUE 7 NOVEMBRE

AVENUE DE L'AMPHITHÉÂTRE

RUE FLORUS

⑦

• Carthage Hannibal Metro Station

KENNEDY

RUE DU PRÉSIDENT

①

Musée National de Carthage

Cathédrale de St-Louis

②

Byrsa Hill

AVENUE HEDI CHAKER

RUE DE CARTHAGE

Citernes de la Malga ④

AVENUE 7 NOVEMBRE

Amphithéâtre des Martyrs ③

RUE TAHA HOUSSINE

0   300 metres
0   300 yards

The Cathédrale de St-Louis is now a cultural centre

4–5

Leaving the cisterns cross rue de Carthage to find two roads forking to the left and right. Take the one on the right. This is rue Mohammed Ali. After 500m you cross a junction and the road changes name to avenue 7 Novembre. Advance another 200m and you will come to the entrance to the **Théâtre d'Hadrian.** There is very little left of the original Roman structure these days but the restored theatre often hosts concerts and plays. Just beyond the entrance to the theatre on the same side of the road is rue Arnobe. Turn left here and this street will lead you to the **Parc Archéologique des Villas Romaines**. If you are a true Roman history buff you will want to venture beyond the Roman villas to explore the Basilique de Damous el Karita. It's not essential, however, because the basilica is quite poorly restored.

Taking a Break

If you followed this walk in its entirety you will certainly be ready for a break. Why not reward yourself with a superb seafood meal at a restaurant nearby? **Le Neptune** is close to both the Thermes d'Antonin Pius and the Carthage Hannibal Metro Station. Overlooking the sea, it's a gem of a restaurant and great value for money.

5–6

After you have visited the Villas Romaines come back to avenue 7 Novembre. Turn left and walk across avenue Habib Bourguiba. You are now in front of the best-preserved Roman site in Carthage, the **Thermes d'Antonin Pius** (▶ 57). You enter through a pleasant garden that leads downhill towards the sea. Make sure you have left enough film in your camera because these Roman baths are probably the most photogenic attraction of all.

6–7

Retrace your path to avenue Habib Bourguiba. Turn left and walk on for 200m, back to the Carthage Hannibal Metro Station.

3 PARC NATIONAL JEBEL ICHKEUL

Drive/Walk

DISTANCE 93km **TIME** 4 hours
START POINT Tunis 🚩 181 D3
END POINT Parc National Jebel Ichkeul
🚩 180 C4

Tunisia's premier national park is set around the beautiful Lac Ichkeul (Lake Ichkeul) in the north of the country. It was designated a UNESCO World Heritage Site in 1977 and shares with the Everglades in Florida the distinction of being the only other site protected as a wetland conservation biosphere reserve. The 89sq km lake below the 511m peak of Jebel Ichkeul makes an ideal stop for migrating birds as it is rich in eels, frogs and mullet. There are several trails within the park, but the main route follows the lakeshore, with some slight detours inland to avoid marshy areas.

1–2

From Tunis follow Route 7 for 75km north-west to the town of **Mateur**. The town was an important objective for the advancing US army during World War II; an important battle was staged here against the occupying

German army. It's also famous throughout Tunisia for its cheese.

2–3

From here, turn right on Route 11 and head north for about 10km until you see the turn-off to the park signposted. If you are travelling from Bizerte head south for 30km on Route 11 and look out for the same turn-off signposted some 9km after the town of **Tinja**.

3–4

The entrance to (Mount Ichkeul National Park) is reached after about 5km and it's on the southeast side of Lac Ichkeul. Here you will be checked in by park rangers and pointed in the direction of the car park. There are no restaurants or hotel facilities within the park's boundaries, and no camping is allowed. Visitors are requested to respect the national park's endangered ecosystem. This is a sanctuary, not a fun park. It is especially important that you do not leave litter behind, and take nothing from the park with you except memories.

Visitors to the Eco-Museum viewing some of Lake Ichkeul's rare birdlife

4–5

About 3km from the car park, up a steep hill, there is a small **Eco-Museum** which explains about the wildlife and ecological importance of the lake. From here you can explore the dirt track, which circles the lake. Colourful kingfishers and flocks of pink flamingos scan

geese, waders, terns, swallows and martins. Other migrants include herons, egrets and white storks. Watch out for the purple gallinule among the reeds, unmistakable with its bright blue plumage and red bill. The indigenous species that live here include stilts, sandpipers and wagtails, as well as birds of prey such as buzzards and eagles. In total, some 100,000 waterfowl are sustained by Lac Ichkeul and its marshes.

Animal life is protected here too, including a herd of water buffalo, descendants of a pair given by the king of Sicily in 1729 to the *bey* (governor) of Tunis. The park is also home to wild boar, jackals, foxes, porcupines, mongooses and otters.

Picnic tables are set up at various places and there are telescopes to view the birds.

the marshes around the lake for prey. They are joined by ducks,

Taking a Break

The park provides **picnic tables** but there are no restaurants, cafés or shops within the sanctuary. It's a delightful place for a picnic, and if you're passing through Mateur buy some of the fresh cheese for which the town is renowned.

Eco-Museum

🕑 Daily 9–12, 1.30–4:30 💰 Inexpensive

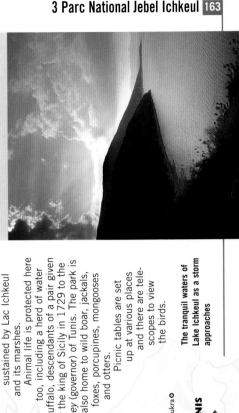

The tranquil waters of Lake Ichkeul as a storm approaches

Bizerte □

Lac de Bizerte

Lac Ichkeul

O Tinja

4 Eco-Museum

Parc National Jebel Ichkeul

3

5

51

11

69

54

56

7

11

2 Mateur

Ariana O

Bardo O

Soukra O

TUNIS

1

7

5

64

0   5 miles
0   10 km

GORGES DE SELJA
Train

In the southwest of the country, between Gafsa (▶ 146) and the famous salt lakes or *chotts* (▶ 136) lies the uninspiring industrial town of Metlaoui. The crowds of people who take the time to visit this town do so for one reason only – to ride the *Lézard Rouge*, the royal train which runs along the cliffs and over the ravines of the Gorges de Selja (Selja Gorge).

Phosphates have been mined in this area since 1885 and a railway track was laid by the French colonialists in 1906 to transport these phosphates out. Some years later, the French presented the *bey* (governor) of Tunis with his very own royal train which could transport him (and apparently his harem!) to his summer palace. The train was known as the *Lézard Rouge* (Red Lizard) because of its colour. The *Lézard Rouge* was refitted with its plush red interior seats in 1995 and the service is now run by **Transtours**.

DISTANCE 46km **TIME** 1 hour
START POINT Metlaoui ✚ 182 B3
END POINT Redeyef ✚ 182 A3

1–2
As you pull out of Metlaoui the train passes a market and a couple of road crossings. A sharp whistle blast scatters donkeys and children and creates general excitement.

You soon find yourself out in the flat, rocky desert. The *Lézard Rouge* then begins climbing the Gorges de Selja. And "gorgeous" they are! You pass through tunnels and look down over 200m ravines at mountain springs below. The **Oued Selja** (River Selja) below is often dry but is subject to flash floods.

The train has an **observation balcony** at the rear. If you have a seat in the rear carriage you should be able to stand outside at some point and appreciate the view; perhaps an ideal photo opportunity.

2–3
The sandstone gorge stretches for some 15km and the town of **Selja** itself lies precariously in the middle. According to local mythology, a

The *Lézard Rouge* stops to allow visitors a closer view of the gorge

hills. You can see the white glint of an occasional mosque on the hilltops.

3–4

From Moulares the views are less dramatic. The train descends into the vast arid plain and soon arrives in Redeyef. If you are returning on the train in the evening, Redeyef's main street has a couple of **small cafés** to while away the time, otherwise there is nothing to see in the town.

Before you go

This journey is particularly popular in the high season so you should definitely **book in advance**. Check with your hotel. The trip only takes an hour and departs every day except Monday at 10:30 am. If you wish to return to Metlaoui that same day the return journey departs Redeyef at 6:30 pm.

Bureau de Lézard Rouge
➕ 182 B3 ✉ Metlaoui ☎ 76 241469; fax: 76 241604 ⏰ Tue–Sun departs: 10:30 am; returns: 6:30 pm 💲 Expensive

Transtours
➕ 179 E2 ✉ 8 rue d'Arabia Saoudite, Tunis ☎ 71 343962; fax: 71 72141

princess once eloped with a warrior who, with one fell swoop of his sword, carved a cleft into the desert rock creating this

huge gorge which he presented as a nuptial bed for his sweetheart.

The train often stops so that passengers can descend and view the surroundings. The scenery on the road to Moulares passes

through a moonscape of sand-coloured hills, often within sight of disused tracks and cars for transporting the phosphate rich earth. The train then enters a flattish plain fringed by

Taking a Break

The *Lézard Rouge* has its own **restaurant carriage** serving mainly snacks.

5 HOUMT SOUQ
Walk

On the north coast of île de Jerba is the beautifully situated town of Houmt Souq. Most visitors to the island spend their time on the lovely beaches of the east coast, but there is definitely more to île de Jerba than just swimming and sunbathing. This pleasant two-hour walk around the island's main town will open your eyes to the unique Jerban culture and point out historical and religious sights that might otherwise go unnoticed. It will then lead you into the fascinating **souq** where you can spend whatever time you like browsing for bargains around the market-place.

DISTANCE 3km **TIME** 2 hours
START POINT Borj el Kebir ✚ 183 E3
END POINT The Souq ✚ 183 E3

mid-15th century when Turkish warriors massacred the Spanish garrison. Today piles of rusting cannonballs stand as mute testimony to those more bloody times. This castle by the sea is just north of the town centre and a good

Borj el Kebir

place to park if you are driving in from the beaches or the *zone touristique*.

If you are here on a Monday or a Thursday there's an open market in the square in front of the Borj el Kebir. With your back to the tower and to the sea, cross the square heading south. Walk straight ahead on rue Taieb Mehiri towards town. After 500m you'll arrive at a junction. Straight across the

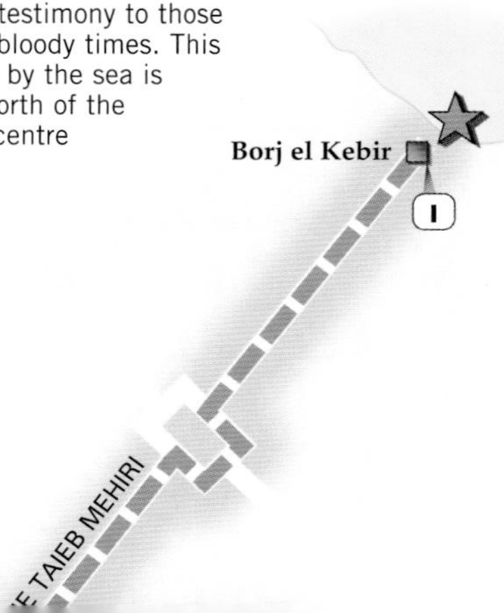

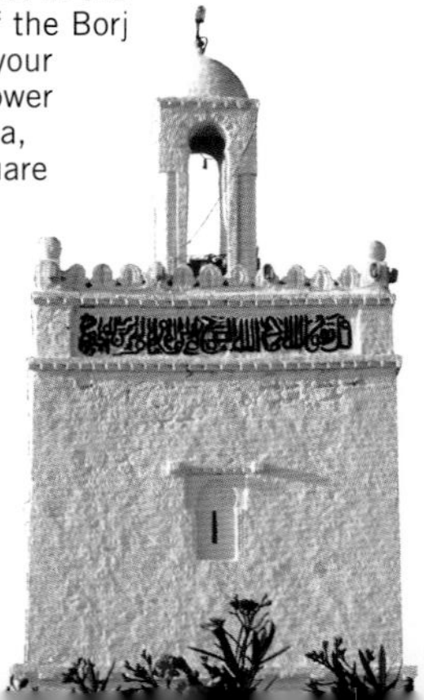

1–2

A good starting place is Houmt Souq's chief monument, the **Borj el Kebir** (▶ 140), the Great Tower. Also known as Borj Ghazi Mustapha, this fortress was the site of a famous battle in the

RUE TAIEB MEHIRI

The solid square tower of the Mosquée des Étrangers

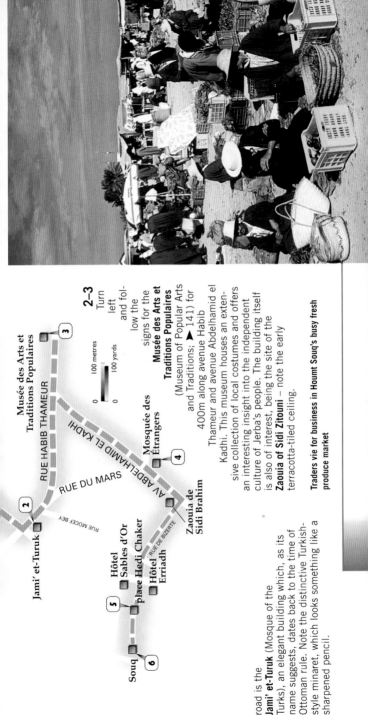

Traders vie for business in **Houmt Souq's** busy fresh produce market

---

Map labels

- Musée des Arts et Traditions Populaires [3]
- RUE HABIB THAMEUR
- Jami' et-Turuk [2]
- RUE DU MARS
- RUE MOCEF BEY
- AV ABDELHAMID EL KADHI
- Mosquée des Étrangers [4]
- Zaouia de Sidi Brahim
- Hôtel Sables d'Or
- place Hedi Chaker
- Hôtel Erriadh
- RUE DE BIZERTE
- Souq [6]
- [5]

0 100 metres
0 100 yards

2–3
Turn left and follow the signs for the **Musée des Arts et Traditions Populaires** (Museum of Popular Arts and Traditions; ▶ 141) for 400m along avenue Habib Thameur and avenue Abdelhamid el Kadhi. This museum houses an extensive collection of local costumes and offers an interesting insight into the independent culture of Jerba's people. The building itself is also of interest, being the site of the **Zaouia of Sidi Zitouni** – note the early terracotta-tiled ceiling.

road is the
Jami' et-Turuk (Mosque of the Turks), an elegant building which, as its name suggests, dates back to the time of Ottoman rule. Note the distinctive Turkish-style minaret, which looks something like a sharpened pencil.

3–4

Retrace your steps for 100m, then follow avenue Abdelhamid el Kadhi as it veers left. Continue to two of Houmt Souq's main historical sights: the 18th-century **Zaouia de Sidi Brahim** and the multi-domed **Mosquée des Étrangers** (Foreigners' Mosque). Both are closed to non-Muslims.

4–5

Turn right at the Zaouia de Sidi Brahim on to rue de Gorès. Continue on until rue Moncef Bey. Cross the road and go straight ahead. Just in front of you, on rue Mohammed el Fergani, is the **Sables d'Or** (▶ 150) on the right and the **Erriadh** (▶ 150) on the left. These are old *funduq*, or *caravanserai*, which have been converted into modern hotels. In times past Arab traders often covered great distances in harsh conditions. Merchants, travellers and pilgrims would therefore seek shelter for the night in a *caravanserai*, or *funduq*, the equivalent of a modern-day motel.

The basic architectural design of the *caravanserai* was an entrance large enough for camels and horses to pass. Inside a courtyard offered stables for the travellers' animals while the guests themselves were housed upstairs in modest sleeping quarters. The proprietors also provided food and water for the weary travellers. *Caravanserai* are known throughout the Muslim world from Morocco to Bangladesh. Nowadays many of these

Two local Jerban women inspect the goods at the fresh produce market

have been converted into modern, camel-free hotels.

5–6

Between these two *caravanserai* rue de Bizerte continues for a couple of hundred metres to a square named place Hedi Chaker. Pass directly through the square and ahead of you is the bustling **souq** or market-place. The winding alleys are packed with goods and products both for locals and tourists. In the squares, carpets are spread seductively on the balustrades over the arcaded walkways, and you will be approached constantly by vendors.

Taking a Break

If you would rather sit and enjoy a delicious meal than go shopping in the *souq*, then you can end your walking tour at place Hedi Chaker. Here you will find **Restaurant du Sud** (▶ 152), which has a terrace leaning out on to the square. It's a perfect spot for people-watching and an excellent rendezvous point if other members of your group or family want to plunge into the *souq* for a while.

Practicalities

BEFORE YOU GO

WHAT YOU NEED

			UK	Germany	USA	Canada	Australia	Ireland	Netherlands	Spain
●	Required	Entry requirements differ depending on your nationality and are also subject to change without notice. Check prior to a visit and follow news events that may affect your situation.								
○	Suggested									
▲	Not required									
△	Not applicable									
Passport/National Identity Card			●	●	●	●	●	●	●	●
Tourist Card (for holiday travel up to 4 weeks, no visa needed)			▲	▲	▲	▲	▲	▲	▲	▲
Onward or Return Ticket			▲	▲	▲	▲	▲	▲	▲	▲
Health Inoculations			○	○	○	○	○	○	○	○
Health Documentation			▲	▲	▲	▲	▲	▲	▲	▲
Travel Insurance			●	●	●	●	●	●	●	●
Driving Licence (national or international)			●	●	●	●	●	●	●	●
Car Insurance Certificate (if own car)			●	●	●	●	●	●	●	●
Car Registration Document (if own car)			●	●	●	●	●	●	●	●

WHEN TO GO

Tunis

High season   Low season

JAN	FEB	MAR	APR	MAY	JUN	JUL	AUG	SEP	OCT	NOV	DEC
26°C	26°C	27°C	29°C	30°C	31°C	32°C	32°C	31°C	29°C	28°C	29°C

☀ Sun   ☁ Cloud   Wet and Windy   Sun/Showers

Northern Tunisia has a typical Mediterranean climate with **hot, dry summers** and **cool, wet winters**. To the west, the Kroumirie and Teboursouk Mountain ranges may sometimes get a light dusting of snow in January. Further south it becomes progressively hotter and drier, especially in the interior away from the coast. **Annual rainfall** ranges from 1,000mm in the north to 180mm in the south. In the interior the Grand Erg Occidental may go without rain for years at a time. In July and August midday temperatures can rise as high as 30°C on the southern coast and touch 45°C in the uninhabited interior. At nights, however, temperatures in the desert tumble and can be unpleasantly cold. Humidity is generally low, especially away from the coast. The **best time to visit** coastal regions is between May and August and the interior during the cooler winter months.

In Canada	In Spain	In France
Tunisian Tourist Office	Oficina Nacional del Turismo	Office National du Tourisme
1253 McGill College, Suite 655	Tunesino, Plaza de Espana 18, Torre de Madrid 28008	Tunisien
Montreal, Quebec H3 B2 Y5	Planta 4, Oficina 1	37 Avenue de l'Operal
☎ (514) 397 1182;	☎ (34-1) 548-1435;	Paris 75002
fax: (514) 397 1647	fax (34-1) 548-3705	☎ (33-1) 4742-7267;
		fax: (33-1) 4742 5268

GETTING THERE

By Air Tunisia has six international airports: Tunis, Monastir, Jerba, Tozeur, Tabarka and Sfax. **Tunis Air** (www.tunisair.com) runs regular scheduled flights to all major European cities and most major European airlines fly to Tunis. There are no direct flights from North America – the simplest route is to fly via **London** or **Paris**.

By Land Although theoretically possible, entry by land from either of Tunisia's neighbours, **Algeria** and **Libya**, is unlikely and impractical at present. At the time of writing the insurgency in Algeria is in apparent decline while Libya is actively seeking to improve relations with the West, so **this may change** in the foreseeable future.

By Sea Regular year-round **ferry services** run to Tunis from both **France** (Marseilles) and **Italy** (Genoa, La Spezia, Naples and Trapani). This is a popular option with European visitors wishing to take their own cars. Both Italian and French ferries are usually booked well in advance.

TIME

Tunisian local time is 1 hour ahead of Greenwich Mean Time (GMT +1) all year round. This means that flying from the UK in summer there is no time difference, while in winter clocks have to be put forward one hour.

CURRENCY AND FOREIGN EXCHANGE

Currency The monetary unit of Tunisia is the dinar which is divided into 1,000 millimes. **Coins** are in denominations of TD1 and 5, 10, 20, 50, 100 and 500 mills. **Notes** are in denominations of TD5, TD10 and TD20. The dinar is a "soft" currency which does not trade on the world currency markets. It's illegal to import or export Tunisian dinars, so visitors cannot obtain Tunisian currency in advance. Within the country US and Canadian dollars, euros and UK pounds are readily accepted for exchange.

Credit cards are widely accepted throughout Tunisia and especially at tourist destinations. Those most commonly in use are Visa and MasterCard. Charge cards such as American Express and Diners Club are less commonly accepted.

Travellers' cheques are readily accepted at most Tunisian banks. The most widely recognised are American Express, Thomas Cook and Visa. The best currencies to use are US dollars, euros or pounds sterling.

Exchange Cash and travellers' cheques can readily be exchanged at most banks and major hotels. Exchange rates are fixed by the Tunisian government, and on leaving the country you can re-exchange 30 per cent of monies changed into dinars up to 100 dinars. ATMs can be found at nearly all banks and are a safe and efficient way of changing money.

TIME DIFFERENCES

GMT	Tunisia	France	Germany	USA (East)	USA (West)
12 noon	1 pm	1 pm	1 pm	7 am	4 am

WHEN YOU ARE THERE

CLOTHING SIZES

UK	Tunisia	USA	
36	46	36	
38	48	38	
40	50	40	
42	52	42	Suits
44	54	44	
46	56	46	
7	41	8	
7.5	42	8.5	
8.5	43	9.5	
9.5	44	10.5	Shoes
10.5	45	11.5	
11	46	12	
14.5	37	14.5	
15	38	15	
15.5	39/40	15.5	
16	41	16	Shirts
16.5	42	16.5	
17	43	17	
8	34	6	
10	36	8	
12	38	10	
14	40	12	Dresses
16	42	14	
18	44	16	
4.5	38	6	
5	38	6.5	
5.5	39	7	
6	39	7.5	Shoes
6.5	40	8	
7	41	8.5	

NATIONAL HOLIDAYS

1 Jan	New Year's Day
18 Jan	Revolution Day
20 Mar	Independence Day
21 Mar	Youth Day
9 Apr	Martyr's Day
1 May	International Labour Day
25 Jul	Republic Day
13 Aug	Women's Day
15 Oct	Evacuation Day
7 Nov	Commemoration Day

In addition to these secular holidays there are also various Muslim fasts and feast days which follow the lunar calendar and move back by 11 days each year (when the moon is sighted). These include the fasting month of **Ramadan**, **'Id al-Fitr** (at the end of Ramadan), **'Id al-Adha** (at the end of the Hajj Pilgrimage) and **Maulid** (the Prophet Muhammad's Birthday).

OPENING HOURS

○ Shops
● Offices
● Banks
● Main Post Offices
● Attractions/Museums
● Pharmacies

8 am 9 am 10 am noon 1 pm 2 pm 4 pm 5 pm 7 pm

☐ Day   ☐ Midday   ☐ Evening

Shops Opening times can be very flexible depending on season, region and individual whim. In the hot season shops may remain closed throughout the afternoon and stay open into the cooler evening. During Ramadan hours are generally shortened. Many **museums** and **historical sites** are closed on Mondays. In larger towns there are 24-hour **pharmacies**.

POLICE 197

FIRE 198

AMBULANCE 481 313/284 808

PERSONAL SAFETY

• Tunisia is generally a very safe country with a relatively low crime rate. What crime there is tends to be petty thievery, and risk of violent attack is low. Be especially careful of pickpockets working with groups of young children who may attempt to distract your attention in some tourist areas.

• Be especially careful of sneak-thievery in crowded *médinas* and *souqs*. Keep cameras and other valuables in closed bags or, if not in use, leave them in the hotel safe.

• Women should not walk around unaccompanied in *médinas* and *souqs* at night. Don't wear revealing clothing, especially in traditional areas – keep it for the beach.

Police assistance:
☎ **197** from any phone

ELECTRICITY

The voltage is generally 220/240 volts, with 110 volts in some remote areas. Sockets accept two round-pin plugs, so an international adaptor is essential for British appliances.

TELEPHONES

The Tunisian telephone system is pretty efficient and continues to improve. In larger towns and cities watch for Taxiphone offices, readily identifiable by bright yellow signs in Arabic and English. Here there will be several booths, shaded from sun and rain and with an attendant to give change. International calls can easily be made using one dinar coins – bring plenty! Some shops have public phones generally indicated by a blue sign.

International Dialling Codes	
UK:	**44**
USA/Canada:	**1**
Germany:	**49**
Spain:	**34**
Netherlands:	**31**
Australia:	**61**

POST OFFICES

All cities and most towns have post offices known as PTTs (Poste, Telephone and Telegraph). Post boxes are usually small and yellow, with Arabic text and PTT in English. Services are average, with postcards and letters to Europe taking around 7 days to arrive.

TIPS/GRATUITIES

Tourist hotel and restaurant charges may include a 10 per cent service charge. Elsewhere the following rates are suggested:

Restaurants	10%
Bars and cafés	10%
Taxis	Optional
Porters, hotel workers	500 mill or 1 dinar
Chambermaids	No
Musicians (restaurants)	500 mill

UK	**USA**	**Canada**	**Germany**	**Spain**
☎ (71) 341444	☎ (71) 782566	☎ (71) 796577	☎ (71) 786455	☎ (71) 782717

HEALTH

 Insurance It's best to take out a travel insurance policy. Major hotels and pharmacists can recommend a reputable doctor when necessary. All treatment must be paid for and then reclaimed from your insurance comapany. If you have to go to hospital, contact your insurance company.

 Dental services All good hotels will be able to recommend a reputable dentist. Any treatment will have to be paid for and then reclaimed on your insurance policy – if possible pay by credit card. Quality of dental service is good, but it's sensible to have a check at home before leaving.

 Weather The sun in Tunis can be fierce at the main beach resorts, in the interior and the deep south. Wear a hat, loose cotton clothing and a high factor sunscreen. Drink plenty of water or fruit juice, avoid too much alcohol, and limit the amount of time spent sunbathing.

 Drugs Pharmacies in Tunisia are generally well stocked. If you require any specialist medication it is wise to take sufficient supplies with you. Pharmacists are well-respected and knowledgeable and can offer helpful practical advice or direct you to a good doctor.

 Safe Water Tap water in Tunisia is generally not safe to drink, so make sure you have a good supply of bottled water, available at hotels, petrol stations and many stores at reasonable prices. Ice in big hotels and resorts should be quite safe to consume, but avoid it in cheap restaurants and cafés.

CONCESSIONS

Students There is a small network of youth hostels in Tunisia. Clean and reasonably priced, they offer a good deal for student travellers. There is an 11 pm curfew and strict segregation of the sexes.

Senior Citizens There are no special concessions for senior citizens, but this is in many ways made up for by the respect with which older people are treated by Tunisians.

TRAVELLING WITH A DISABILITY

There are relatively few facilities for travellers with disabilities in Tunisia, though a few of the major monuments have access ramps, and many resorts and hotels have wheelchair access to some rooms and most amenities. If you have special requirements, check these details carefully before making a reservation.

CHILDREN

As with people everywhere, Tunisians love children, and if you are travelling with them it will bring you many chance encounters with the locals. All-inclusive resorts have childcare facilities and lots of activities for kids, which makes this type of holiday so popular with families.

TOILETS

Public toilets are few and are not usually very clean. When away from your hotel discard toilet paper in the bin provided.

CUSTOMS

The import of wildlife souvenirs sourced from rare or endangered species may be either illegal or require a special permit. Before buying, check your home country's customs regulations.

USEFUL WORDS AND PHRASES

The official language in Tunisia is Arabic, though French is also widely spoken, as is an often confusing mixture of Arabic and French. The Arabic of Tunisia (as well as Algeria and Morocco) is called Maghribi ("of the sunset") and is very different to classical Arabic. Vowels tend to be fore-shortened or dropped altogether, and there's a considerable admixture of French and Italian terms. In the larger cities French is widely spoken, but in smaller towns and the countryside a little Arabic will both get you around and also be much appreciated.

GREETINGS AND COMMON WORDS

Yes **Na'am, iyeh**

No **La**

Please **Minfadlak**

Thank you (very much) **Shukran (jazilan)**

Don't mention it **La shukran 'ala wajib**

Hello (to Muslims) **As salaam alaykum**

Response (to Muslims) **Wa alaykum salaam**

Hello (informal) **La bes**

Response **Bikheer**

Welcome **Ahlan wa sahlan, marhaba**

Response **Ahlan bik**

Goodbye **Ma'asalaama, bislemah**

Good morning **Sabah al-kheir**

Good morning (*response*) **Sabah an-nur**

Good evening **Misa al-kheir**

Good evening (*response*) **Misa an-nur**

Good night **Tesbah al-kheir**

How are you? **Kayf halak?**

Fine, thank you **Bikheer alhamdulillah**

God willing **Inshallah**

Excuse me **Samahni**

What is your name? **Ma'howa ismok?**

My name is... **Ismi howa...**

Do you speak English? **Tatakallem ingliz?**

It doesn't matter **Ma'alesh**

How much? **Kadesh?**

Too expensive **Yessir**

I understand **Fhemt**

I don't understand **Ma fhemtesh**

Go away! **Imshee!**

Good **Behi**

Bad **Mush behi**

Why **Laysh?**

Let's go! **Hay bina!**

ACCOMMODATION

Where is...? **Feyn...?**

the hotel **Al Otel**

the restaurant **Al Mataam**

the toilet **El mirhadh / et toilette**

the pharmacy **Es saydaliyya**

How much is a room per night? **Kamel ghorfa el-layla?**

Could I see a room? **Mumkin shouf al–ghorfa?**

With two beds (twin) **Ma zouz afresh**

Air-conditioned **Klimatizasiyon**

Shower **Dush**

Hot water **Ma sekhouna**

This is fine **Hada bahi**

DAYS

Sunday **yawm al-ahad**

Monday **yawm al-itnayn**

Tuesday **yawm al-talaat**

Wednesday **yawm al-arbah**

Thursday **yawm al-khamees**

Friday **yawm al-jumah**

Saturday **yawm as-sabt**

Yesterday **Ams**

Today **Al yawm**

Tomorrow **Bukra**

DIRECTIONS AND TRAVELLING

I want to go to... **Urid ana adhaba illa...**

What is the fare to...? **Mahowa assir illa...?**

To the left **Al yassar**

To the right **Al yameen**

Straight on **Ala toul**

Stop here, please **Qif honamen minfadlak**

Airport **Al mataar**

Bus station **Mahattat al otobis**

Train station **Mahattat al tran**

Ticket office **Maktab al tazkara**

Car **Sayara**

Taxi **Teksi**

Petrol **Benzeen**

Puncture **Tokob**

Ferry **Al Ferri**

NUMBERS

0 sifr	6 sitta	12 itnash	18 tmantash
1 wahid	7 sabaa	13 talatash	19 tissatash
2 itnayn	8 tamania	14 arbatash	20 ishreen
3 talaata	9 tissa	15 khamstash	30 tlateen
4 arba'a	10 ashra	16 sittash	100 mia
5 khams	11 ihdash	17 sabatash	1,000 alf

MENU READER

aubergine **ibdanzhal**	chickpeas **hummus**	fruit **fawakih**	salad **shlada**
barbeque **shshwa**	chickpea soup	juice **'asir**	salt **milh**
beans **lubya**	**lablabi**	lamb **allush**	semolina **couscous / seksu**
beef **baqri**	coffee **qahwa**	lentils **l'adess**	soup **shorba**
beer **birra**	croissant	meat **lahm**	sugar **sukar**
boiled **ghalla**	**krwassa**	milk **halib**	tea **shai**
bread **khubz**	egg **'adham**	olive **zaitoun**	vegetables
butter **zebda**	fish **samak**	pepper **felfel**	**khodra**
cheese **zhben**	French fries	pepper sauce	water **maa**
chicken **djaj**	**batata maklya**	**harissa**	wine **sharab**
		potato **batata**	

RESTAURANT

Breakfast **Futoor**	Enough **Izzi**
Lunch **Ada**	I'm a vegetarian
Dinner **Asha**	**Makanakulsh laham**
Waiter **Garson**	Delicious **Lathith**
Menu **Menu**	Bill, the **Al hisaab**

GLOSSARY

Aïn Spring
Allah God
Bab Gate
Bayt House
Bey Governor
Bir Well
Borj Tower or fort
Burnous Hooded cape
Chechia Red felt hat
Chicha Water pipe
Chott Salt lake
Dar Town house or palace
Dey Governor
Funduq Caravanserai
Ghar Cave
Ghurfa Rock or mud chambers
Hajj Pilgrimage to Mecca
Hammam Public bath
Hijab Veil or headscarf
Id al Adha Feast marking end of Hajj
Id al Fitr Feast marking end of Ramadan
Islam Submission (to God's will)
Jebel Mountain
Kasbah Citadel
Kilim Woven Berber rug
Koubba Dome, saint's tomb
Ksar Fortified village
Maghreb Northwest Africa
Malouf Traditional Tunisian music

Marabout Holy man
Masjid Mosque
Medersa, madrassa Islamic school
Mergoum Carpet with geometric designs
Medersa Islamic school
Médina (Old) city
Mihrab Niche in mosque indicating Qibla
Muezzin He who gives the call to prayer
Oued River, dry river bed
Qibla Direction of prayer (Mecca)
Qur'an Holy book of Islam
Ramadan Month of fasting
Ribat Fortified stronghold
Sahel The coast
Sharia Islamic Law
Sidi A saint
Souq Market
Sufi Islamic mystic
Tourbet Mausoleum
Zawiyya, zaouia Shrine, saint's tomb

IF YOU NEED HELP

Help! **Aktooni!**
Police **Shurta /Bolees**
Fire **Afia**
Hospital **Mustashfa**
Doctor **Tabeeb / Duktoor**

Atlas

180/181

Bulla Regia

TUNIS
178/179

SOUSSE
186

Sbeïtla

Sfax

Île de Jerba

182/183

Matmata

184/185

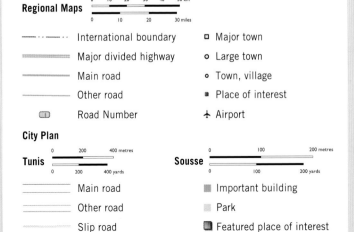

Regional Maps

| 0 | 10 | 20 | 30 | 40 | 50 km |

| 0 | 10 | 20 | 30 miles |

— ·· — ··   International boundary

▭ Major town

▬▬▬▬   Major divided highway

○ Large town

———   Main road

○ Town, village

———   Other road

▪ Place of interest

▭   Road Number

✈ Airport

City Plan

| 0 | 200 | 400 metres |

| 0 | 200 | 400 yards |

Tunis

| 0 | 100 | 200 metres |

| 0 | 100 | 200 yards |

Sousse

———   Main road

▪ Important building

———   Other road

▪ Park

∼∼∼∼   Slip road

▪ Featured place of interest

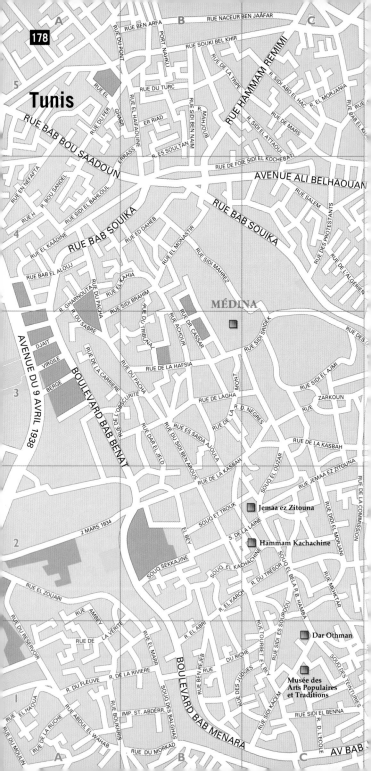

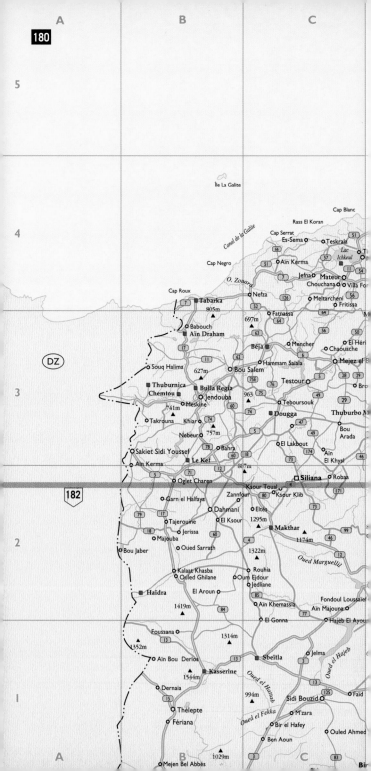

Rass Engelah
■ Cap Bizerte
■ Bizerte
Lac
de Bizerte
inja
Menzel Bourguiba
Gournata o
Utica ■ Raf Raf Plage
■ Rass Sidi Ali el-Mekki
Île Zembra
Cap Bon
69
7
Bach Hamba
Golfe de Tunis
El Haouaria
27 Dar Allouch
■ Kerkouane
Ariana o
8
Soukra o ■ Gammarth
■ La Marsa
Rass
el Fartass
Zaoulet El-Mgaiez
Tazoghrane
45 ■ Kelibia
Musée du Bardo ■
Ville Nouvelle ■
The Médina ■ ■ Sidi Bou Saïd
✈ ■ Carthage
■ La Goulette
TUNIS
26
Mraïssa
Menzel Temime
55 5
Mohammedia o
Soliman o ■ Menzel Bouzelfa
34 Lebna
Bab
40
37 Khelidia
Oudna
Grombalia
Korba
27
Ain Saf-Saf
El M'Nagha
El Maâmoura
Tazerka
ough
333
36 35
Bou Argoub
■ Nabeul
Moghrane o
28
Hammamet
Majus
■ Zaghouan
Seguermess o
Pupput
El Fahs
4
133 35 Salloum
Draa Ben Jouider o Jeradou
Golfe
de
Hammamet
132
988m ▲
Saouaf
Ain Er Rahma
Ouled Abdallah o Enfidaville
Bir Chaouach

Ouled Ameur
183
El Jema
Koundar o S. Bou Ali
Golfe de Monastir
Sbikha o El Alam
2 Kaala Kebira o ■ Port el Kantaoui
816m ▲
3
Kaala Sghira o ■ Sousse
Ain Jloula
82 ■ Monastir
Rouissed
M'saken o ✈
El Batlen o ■ Kairouan
100 El Onk
Ksibet El Mediouni
Cherichira o
Regueda
Bourjine o Jemmel o Teboulba
Rass Dimass
Zeramdine o
86 2 Zaafrana
M'Zougha o Cherahil
■ Mahdia
Cap Afrique
Menzel Mehiri o
87 Bou Merdès
Ksour Essaf o Salakta
Rass Salatka
Nasr Allah o
Souassi o
26 Tielsa
87 El Bhira
644m ▲
81 Ouled Achor
Chorbane ■ El Jem
Zorda
El Bradâa
Guedabna
73
Bir Remadhiaia o
Chebba
Souq Hibira
Mellouleche
Rass Kaboudia
Bou Thadi o
119 El Hencha
Ouled Bou Smir
655m ▲
Limaya o Ksar Errih
Bir Tebeug
82 Rass Bou Tria
Louza
Ouled Hafous
96
Dokhane o El Amra
Menzel Chaker
13 81
El Bedarna
Reguieb o
El Aouabed
Mansour
■ Îles Kerkennah
19
Ech-Chergui o El Ataya
Ali Ben Khelifa ■
14 Magda Agareb o Sfax
Remla o El Abassia

D E F

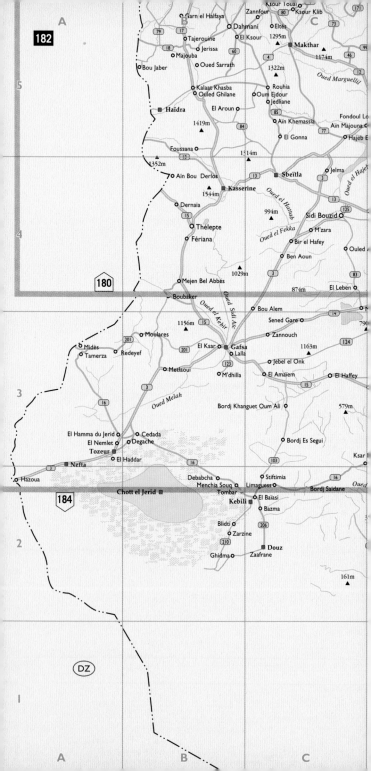

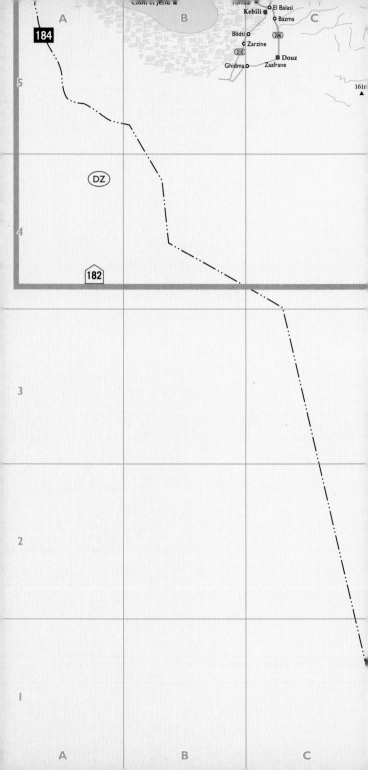

A

B

C

5

DZ

4

3

2

I

A

B

C

Tombar

Kebili

El Baïasi

Bazma

206

Blidti

Zarzine

210

Ghidma

Zaafrane

Douz

Chott el Jerid

161r

A

B

C

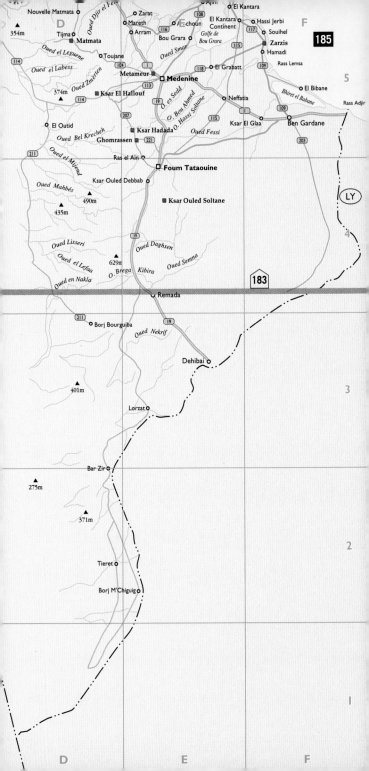

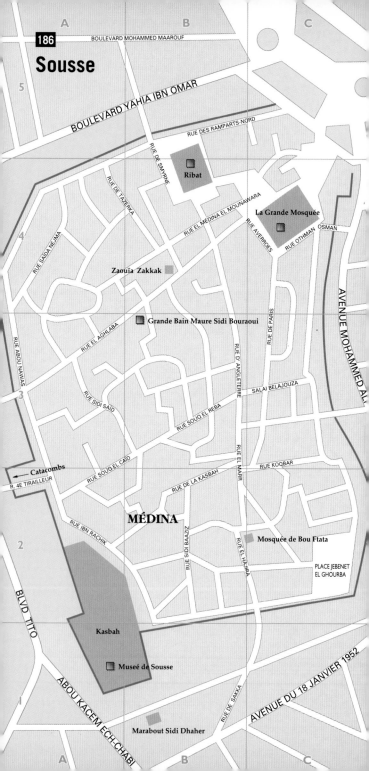

Sousse

BOULEVARD MOHAMMED MAAROUF

BOULEVARD YAHIA IBN OMAR

RUE DES RAMPARTS-NORD

RUE DE SMYRNE

RUE DE TAZERKA

Ribat

La Grande Mosquée

RUE EL MÉDINA EL MOUNAWARA

RUE AVERROÈS

RUE OTHMAN

OSMAN

AVENUE MOHAMMED ALI

RUE SAIDA NEJMA

Zaouïa Zakkak

Grande Bain Maure Sidi Bouraoui

RUE EL AGHLABA

RUE D' ANGLETERRE

RUE DE PARIS

RUE ABOU NAWAS

RUE SIDI SAÏD

SALAI BELAJOUZA

RUE SOUQ EL REBA

Catacombs

R. 4E TIRAILLEUR

RUE SOUQ EL CAID

RUE EL MAIR

RUE KOQBAR

RUE DE LA KASBAH

MÉDINA

RUE IBN RACHIK

Mosquée de Bou Ftata

RUE SIDI BAAZIZ

RUE EL HAJRA

PLACE JEBENET EL GHOURBA

BLVD TITO

Kasbah

Museé de Sousse

ABOU KACEM ECH-CHABI

RUE DE SAKKA

AVENUE DU 18 JANVIER 1952

Marabout Sidi Dhaher

Picture credits

The Automobile Association wishes to thank the following photographers, libraries and museums for their assistance with the preparation of this book.
Front and back cover: all images AA World Travel Library/Steve Day
BRIDGEMAN ART LIBRARY 12bl Admiral Khair-ed-din (c.1465-1546) 1540, Reis Haydar, Nakkep, called Nigari (1494–1572)/Topkapi Palace Museum, Istanbul, Turkey, 16/17 The Death of Dido (oil on canvas), Sacchi, Andrea (1599–1661)/Musee des Beaux-Arts, Caen, France, Giraudon/Bridgeman Art Library, 18/19 Hannibal Crossing the Alps (fresco), Ripanda, Jacopo (fl.1490–1530)/Pinacoteca Capitolina, Palazzo Conservatori, Rome, Italy, 24t Gustave Flaubert (1821–1880) (b/w photo), Nadar, (Gaspard Felix Tournachon) (1820-1910)/Private Collection, CREDIT: Ken Welsh, 28/29b Gold plate with Phoenician inscription, from Santa Severa, Pyrgi, 5th century BC/Museo Archeologico di Villa Giulia, Rome, Italy. IMPERIAL WAR MUSEUM 22/23(c), 22/23(b), 23(t). MAGNUM PHOTOS 20(t). MARY EVANS PICTURE LIBRARY 13(tr), 17, 21, 24(b), 25. NATIONAL MARITIME MUSEUM 14/15. TUNISIA NATIONAL TOURIST OFFICE 6/7(bg), 21(bg), 22/23(bg). WORLD PICTURES 3(cb), 9(tr), 155, 165.
The remaining photographs are held in the Association's own photo library (AA World Travel Library) and were taken by Steve Day, with the exception of 10/11 which was taken by Steve McBride.
Abbreviations for terms appearing above: (t) top; (b) bottom; (l) left; (r) right; (c) centre (bg) background.

Questionnaire

Dear Traveller
Your comments, opinions and recommendations
are very important to us. So please help us to improve
our travel guides by taking a few minutes to complete
this simple questionnaire.

You do not need a stamp (unless posted outside the UK). If you do not
want to remove this page from your guide, then photocopy it or write your
answers on a plain sheet of paper.

Send to: The Editor, Spiral Guides, AA World Travel Guides,
FREEPOST SCE 4598, Basingstoke RG21 4GY.

Your recommendations...
We always encourage readers' recommendations for restaurants, night-life or shopping
– if your recommendation is used in the next edition of the guide, we will send you a
FREE AA Spiral Guide of your choice. Please state below the establishment name,
location and your reasons for recommending it.

_____

_____

_____

_____

_____

Please send me AA Spiral _____
(see list of titles inside the back cover)

About this guide...
Which title did you buy?

_____ **AA Spiral**

Where did you buy it? _____

When? m m / y y

Why did you choose an AA Spiral Guide? _____

_____

_____

_____

Did this guide meet your expectations?

Exceeded ☐   Met all ☐   Met most ☐   Fell below ☐

Please give your reasons _____

_____

_____

_____

_____

continued on next page...

Were there any aspects of this guide that you particularly liked?

Is there anything we could have done better?

About you...

Name (Mr/Mrs/Ms)

Address

Postcode

Daytime tel no   email

Please *only* give us your email address and mobile phone number if you wish to hear from us about other products and services from the AA and partners by email or text or mms.

Which age group are you in?

Under 25 ☐   25–34 ☐   35–44 ☐   45–54 ☐   55–64 ☐   65+ ☐

How many trips do you make a year?

Less than one ☐   One ☐   Two ☐   Three or more ☐

Are you an AA member? Yes ☐   No ☐

About your trip...

When did you book? mm/ y y   When did you travel? mm/ y y

How long did you stay?

Was it for business or leisure?

Did you buy any other travel guides for your trip?   ☐ Yes   ☐ No

If yes, which ones?

Thank you for taking the time to complete this questionnaire. Please send it to us as soon as possible, and remember, you do not need a stamp (unless posted outside the UK).
